C0-AZQ-288

FUND RAISING

for Human Service Agencies

Roberta Nelson-Walker

High Tide Press
Homewood, IL

A HIGH TIDE BOOK

Published by High Tide Press Inc.

3650 West 183rd Street, Homewood, Illinois 60430

www.hightidepress.com / toll-free: 1-888-487-7377

Copyright ©2005 by Roberta Nelson-Walker

All rights reserved under International
and Pan-American Copyright Conventions

Fund Raising for Social Service Agencies /
by Roberta Nelson-Walker – 1st ed.

ISBN: 1-892696-33-9

Printed in the United States of America

This book is dedicated to people who give of themselves to others and thereby truly express and experience love.

TABLE OF CONTENTS

ACKNOWLEDGEMENTS

My warmest thanks are for my dear husband Clay Klein, who provides inspiration, encouragement and support as well as thoughtful, constructive suggestions.

I am also deeply grateful for all those wonderful human beings who give their lives and time willingly as professionals and volunteers to make the world a better place, improving the quality of life for people who face special challenges.

My deepest gratitude goes to those who are a source of daily, personal inspiration: Father Howard Lincoln, Father Barry Brunsman and Father John Lenoir. We thank our Lord every day for the gifts we have and our ability to share.

I greatly admire Audrey, Barbara, Carol, Jerry, Yasmin and many others whose exemplary dedication to philanthropy and volunteer support make life joyful.

As a professional, I thank Art Dykstra, Executive Director Extraordinaire, and the editors of this book. All the profits from the sale of this book are used to help support programs which serve people with disabilities.

1

CHARITABLE GIVING: AN INTRODUCTION

Giving and sharing have a long history. The concepts appear most prominently as integral parts of religious and moral belief systems throughout the world. The majority of religions promote the concept of sharing and giving in thanksgiving, while many others also advocate tithing, the practice of dedicating ten percent of one's income to good works. In the Judeo-Christian tradition, charitable giving has evolved from the Mosaic law that commanded farmers to leave the gleanings in the fields. Leviticus 19:10 contains the specific mandate: "Likewise you shall not pick your vineyard bare, nor gather up the grapes that have fallen. These things you shall leave for the poor and the alien." As a result, many people have given to the church and also shared their surplus with others.

> Fund raising is
> the gentle art
> of teaching
> the joy of giving.
>
> Hank Rosso

The ancient Greeks and Romans each had their own approaches to a sense of responsibility for the destitute, orphans and aliens. In Greece, "the laws of social life as stated by Hesiod about 700 B.C. are comparatively simple. The groundwork of Hesiod's charity is neighborly help, but this help is limited in character insofar as the community is concerned. A beggar is expected to do some sort of work in return for food and shelter."[1] Aristotle criticized simply giving money to the poorer citizens and suggested that the direction in which reform must be sought is "to contrive that poverty should become temporary and not permanent." He proposed that public aid and voluntary charity should be given in large enough amounts that people could purchase small farms or start businesses. The famous Roman, Cicero, said that three conditions should be met in regard to giving, which indicate the deed and its purpose:

- Not to do harm to the person one would benefit
- Not to exceed one's means
- To have regard to merit.[2]

Through the centuries, religious organizations ministered to the needs of the poor with donations from their members. There were monasteries, hospitals and orphanages. People also gave bread and alms to needy individuals when they came to the door. This pattern was emulated in the United States when in the nineteenth century, large numbers of immigrants came to the country. In addition, new organizations were founded to deal with the issues of feeding, housing and educating victims of the European famines and droughts.[3]

During the late nineteenth and early twentieth centuries, Andrew Carnegie and John Rockefeller were the giants of what seemed a golden age. Their pattern of giving elevated charity to philanthropy. Andrew Carnegie believed that "the man who dies rich dies disgraced." In fact, he disposed of 90 percent of his vast fortune by the end of his life.[4]

The Great Depression of the late 1920s and 1930s crystallized the argument for citizen entitlement to basic services from the government, when the vast majority of breadwinners lost their jobs and these normally self-supporting individuals became dependent on others for food and shelter. The magnitude of the problem drove the creation of many of the programs associated with immediate emergency relief for the millions of unemployed people who could no longer be taken care of by private charity or state and local funds. This was the beginning of President Franklin D. Roosevelt's New Deal, which instituted the Federal Emergency Relief Act. It was followed by various acts to create jobs for the unemployed at federal expense, such as the Civilian Conservation Corps, the Civil Works Administration and the Works Progress Administration. Over the years, those acts led to the government-funded programs for social welfare that we have in the United States today. These include unemployment insurance, public health and welfare for the poorest sector of our population as well as Social Security for the senior population and people with disabilities. Depending on the political party in power in Washington, programs to create jobs when the economy is faltering may or may not be a priority.

Tax Laws Encouraging Charitable Giving

Some tax laws were already in place in the 1930s to encourage philanthropy and charitable giving, though they have gradually been changed over time in recognition of their positive impact. The amended rules generally continue to provide tax incentives to those who contribute to a special class of organizations (nonprofits), qualified as 501(c)3 by the Internal Revenue Service (IRS) Code.

Sometimes, people use the word nonprofit interchangeably with "public charity"; however, there is a difference between them. The term "nonprofit" or "tax exempt organization" refers to a large category of organizations that are exempt from federal income tax and often from state and local sales taxes as well as property taxes. They do not all qualify for the same treatment of contributions that is available to a 501(c)3 public charity.

The IRS code includes more than twenty categories of nonprofit organizations. Among them are civic leagues [501(c)4]; labor, agricultural or horticultural organizations [501(c)5]; business leagues [501(c)6]; and clubs organized for pleasure, recreation or other nonprofit purposes [501(c)7]. In this book, we use the word "charity" and "charitable organizations" to refer to entities that provide services and have 501(c)3 status. This status is extremely valuable because it entitles donors to the most advantageous type of deductions for their contributions. For instance, IRS Code Section 170(b)(1)(D) states that gifts of qualified appreciated stock are fully deductible up to the fair market value. Donors can also deduct the full market value of other appreciated property as well. Therefore, when a donor is considering a significant contribution, his or her professional advisors (attorneys, accountants and financial planners) always want to see the "letter" granted by the IRS, ruling that the entity is entitled to 501(c)3 status.

From Charity to Philanthropy

A great many people still believe in "giving to charity" in just those terms. Their wish is to share their bounty with people less fortunate, whether they themselves are at the poverty level or well-to-do. They give directly to people in need although there is no tax benefit to them, and they give spontaneously to organizations that touch them. The *American Heritage Dictionary* defines this type of giving as charity. "1. The provision of help or relief to the poor; almsgiving. 2. Something that is given to help the needy; alms. 3. An institution, organization, or fund established to help the needy."[5]

Philanthropy, on the other hand, is an organized means of giving with specific goals in mind. It is often money given to change the social situation that causes the problem. The *American Heritage Dictionary* defines it as: "an action or institution designed to promote human welfare."[6]

> Acts of kindness
> are constant.
> The memory
> of each act
> endures for years.
>
> Vera Waters

In a 1993 lecture to the Planned Giving Institute of the College of William and Mary in Williamsburg, Virginia, Robert Gross defined the difference more eloquently. He differentiates charity and philanthropy as two discrete movements within the broader rubric of "humanitarianism." Charity, he argues, "expresses an impulse to personal service." In contrast, philanthropy "seeks not so much to aid individuals as to reform society by eliminating the problems of society that beset particular persons; philanthropy aims to usher in a world where charity is uncommon–and perhaps unnecessary." As a result, Gross also calls for the reintegration of the charitable spirit into discussions of public philanthropy.[7]

In an effort to address the financial concerns of wealthy young people who are interested in using their assets effectively, Tracy Gary and Melissa Kohner have written a book called *Inspired Philanthropy*. In it, they advocate creating a giving plan rather than just responding to requests for donations. The book gives specific steps that potential donors can use to align their most important wishes with where and how they give their money, talent and time. Their stated beliefs about inspired philanthropy include:

- Everyone has a role in changing the inequities of society, regardless of income or class.
- Philanthropy is a creative expression of that part of yourself that cares about and believes in the potential for change.
- The most effective philanthropy joins your interests and experiences with the current needs in your community and seeks desired outcomes.
- Thoughtful, planned giving gives you a chance to express yourself and your passion as well as your goals and reasons for giving.
- Creating a giving plan fosters more enjoyment, ingenuity and effectiveness in personal philanthropy than automatic, reactive giving.
- Coming into your own true place of giving is an evolving, definable and developmental process.
- Inspired philanthropy and service have transforming powers for all–givers and receivers.[8]

In spite of definitions and explanations of intent, many professionals in human service fields continue to have a negative reaction to the word "charity" because it connotes the use of what is left over for the needy, rather than encouraging them to find ways to be self-sufficient. In reality, some people still respond to the opportunity to take care of their fellow men through charitable giving while others prefer philanthropy. It is unlikely either approach will ever become the only way.

This book is meant to help people active in charitable organizations use their resources more effectively. It is written to enable readers to turn to the areas of greatest interest first or read the whole book through–whichever best meets their needs.

2

BUILDING THE HUMAN SERVICE AGENCY

Generally speaking, building a strong human service agency begins with a few people who recognize a need and recruit others to be on the board of a new organization. With the help of an attorney, the board crafts the articles of incorporation and determines the mission of the agency. Board members then hire an executive director, who in turn recruits and trains a management team to raise the resources the organization needs to carry out its segment of the mission. The process sounds deceptively uncomplicated, but in reality it often takes years to find the resources to supply the need.

Currently, funding a viable human service agency requires a great deal of time and research. Fortunately, resources are available for creating and managing nonprofits, so even the very small organizations should not lose heart.

> Life is an echo;
> what you send out
> comes back.
>
> Author unknown

Building Strong Leadership

Thomas E. Broce, an authority on fund raising, maintains that all the principles of fund raising for small social service agencies are the same as those for large organizations such as universities. A top priority, he says, should be placed on building board strength. However, finding appropriate board members is not a simple matter. Often, those who seem to be promising candidates do not contribute what is expected when they actually take a board position. To help solve the problem, some organizations choose leadership candidates from satellite support groups. For example, an effective campaign chairperson could easily contribute excellent ideas and fund-raising strategies in a governance position. Public institutions such as state universities, library districts and historical places have governing board members that are either elected or appointed. These board members are more likely to be "watchdogs for the public" than people concerned with fund raising. In these instances, the organizations may establish a foundation whose purpose is to govern and oversee the stewardship program.[1]

Human service agencies have yet another challenge. In most instances, the initial sources of funding are tax based, so their boards have not developed the connections and agency supports necessary to make private contributions a major source of funds. Establishing a foundation whose board members are geared toward generating private contributions can broaden an organization's funding base, reducing its dependency on fluctuating government subsidies.

Even small, community nonprofit organizations can use the same technique of establishing a support foundation when their boards are "working boards" of individuals, who are not affluent but do contribute time and talent. The foundation can allow room for inviting new board members who can contribute financially, and have enough influence on others in the community that when they ask for donations, people are willing to give.

Creating Community Support through Fund Raising

One of the major problems that human service agencies face is the negative views that many people have toward persons with mental retardation, cerebral palsy, epilepsy, mental illness, addiction issues and other physical or psychological disabilities. Although there is less rejection of people with disabilities than was common 20 or 30 years ago, the shift in attitudes has not been sufficient to provide full employment opportunities and community acceptance for many of the individuals served by these agencies.

Fortunately, fund raising can be used to strengthen the human service agency. Used as a tool, fund-raising activities educate the community about the need that the agency fills and the people it serves. When community members learn about the agency's mission and get involved in its work, negative attitudes begin to change, and the community begins to do a better job of incorporating individuals with disabilities.

John W. Gardner, founding chairman of Common Cause and co-founder of Independent Sector, addresses some of these issues in his book *Building Community*. In "Steps Toward Solutions," he lists some of the elements that can result in changing community attitudes.

Among the conditions that enhance the possibility of participation are the following:

- A community culture that enables all members and all subgroups to feel accepted and confident that their needs will be considered.
- Free and responsible media of communication.
- Avoidance of the delusion that experts and professionals will solve all problems—what some have called managerial liberalism—making citizen action unnecessary.
- A strong tradition of public service.[2]

Gardner notes that those who participate choose to do so themselves, so participation is never total. Some have more interest in participating, while others have more of the energy that participation requires. Therefore, a small group of activists who dominate will emerge, and the larger group will play less directive roles.[3]

Influencing those in power to create change requires the participation of individual citizens. Leaders listen to people in their community, and they heed the words of people they respect even more carefully. A real demonstration of financial support for a local public benefit organization catches their attention particularly when it is accompanied by letters and verbal comments from constituents who participated. Business leaders who see the names of supporters are also more apt to take an active role in doing what they can to support the efforts of the organization. Their contributions may include monetary donations, sponsoring an event, donating goods and services, and/or expanding or redefining their job descriptions to make it easier to hire people with special challenges. Clearly, broad participation creates awareness and change.

It is often said that friend raising precedes fund raising. A fund-raising or community education volunteer can be an advocate for the organization wherever he goes in the normal course of daily activities. In fact, it is easier for such a volunteer to talk with people about the organization for which he has a passion in one-on-one situations at work or at social events. His enthusiasm is contagious and the stories of successes and challenges faced by the charity can be powerful tools for social action.

Fund raising should be considered one of the tools for social change. As volunteers in the community learn of the barriers to housing or employment for people with disabilities, they often put the wheels in motion to create a more open environment for hiring possibilities. The wife, husband, or other family member who talks to his or her family or friends about situations he or she considers unfair can spark a beneficial chain reaction. The listener may be concerned enough to talk with a friend who can make a difference in the situation.

In fact, the more people talk about problems in the community, the greater the likelihood that the issue will reach the ears of decision makers who can help bring about change. As decision makers at higher and higher levels hear the story from persons they respect, the likelihood rises that changes will be made. Similarly, if enough people in the community act to correct problems in one or two instances, others may see that such changes can happen in a broader realm.

Community education, friend raising, and fund raising are not about begging for money. They are about helping to create understanding and providing the resources that open new opportunities. Those who are thankful for what they enjoy can help pave the way for people with fewer opportunities to maximize their own development. It is true that some people care only about themselves and their own needs, but the vast majority of individuals feel good when they are helping others.

Building the Volunteer Base

Recruiting people who are interested in helping others is important for the service agency. Some may be interested in opportunities for direct volunteer work. In these cases, program managers need to weigh the advantages and disadvantages of using volunteers in these capacities. The managers may find that recruiting, training and scheduling volunteers is a great deal of work. In addition, certain funding grants are very specific about staffing ratios and the qualifications of those giving services. However, properly trained volunteers provide extra hands, eyes and ears to give valuable, individual attention.

If the program managers or the volunteers themselves are uncomfortable with providing programmatic support, there are always opportunities for volunteers to work in community outreach and fund raising. Since these areas are absolutely essential to the existence of the agency, volunteers can know that they are contributing to the success of both the agency and the people it serves.

A priest, who is now well into his eighties, told a story that emphasizes the value of service. He recounted the experience of another officer who had served in the Dutch Navy. The man had been a prisoner of war during World War II and found the Catholic faith during his internment. He survived the time in the camp and rose to the rank of admiral after the war. One day he and fellow officers, including a group of retired officers, were having a celebration in the dining room on board a ship. During the event, someone noticed that the most revered and decorated retired admiral was sitting at the end of the room looking very tearful. When asked the reason for his sadness, he said, "Look at the stewards who serve us. They have the gold. The ability to serve is the gold, and I can no longer do it."[4]

> Love and gratitude are fundamental to the phenomenon of life in all of nature.
>
> Masaru Emoto

The staff and administrators of the human service agency must remember that they are not begging the haves to give to the have-nots; they are offering them the privilege of serving.

Building the Constituency

The constituency consists of the clients, families of clients, staff, volunteers, donors and friends of the organization. Maintaining the service agency's current constituency and recruiting more people are important cornerstones of developing agency support. The following questions may offer some avenues through which agency personnel can continue to draw people to the cause.

- In addition to a newsletter and invitations to special events, how do you recruit new volunteers and donors?
- Do you send press releases to the newspapers to publicize a specific need?
- Do your volunteers and staff let people know that there are volunteer opportunities?
- When you have staff positions to fill, you place ads in the newspaper; but do you do the same for volunteer positions?
- Is there a Welcome Wagon organization or a Newcomer's Club in town that the agency can access for more potential volunteers and donors?
- Do you have a brochure that lists ways people can get involved?
- Do you have a volunteer chairperson who communicates with clubs and other organizations about specific needs?
- Is there a specific staff member who oversees volunteer opportunities?
- Does a specific staff member keep in touch with the families of clients served?
- Do the two staff members talk to each other?
- Do you hold regular open houses and actively recruit people to attend?

A Permanent Sense of Belonging

Any organization that has alumni would be wise to keep in touch with the people it has served and with those who have helped them carry out their mission. That translates into maintaining a database of clients or students as well as volunteers and donors. The task of keeping a database current is an enormous responsibility and requires an annual devoted review by everyone who can possibly be involved. The issues of confidentiality and privacy make it a complicated but not insurmountable task.

Opportunities for Further Involvement

Often, donors who give their time or money work in relative isolation, seeing the same staff and volunteers week after week. In the case of financial donors, some never see anyone. What type of events does the organization sponsor that would offer social and informational opportunities to keep people in touch with the agency's latest work? Open houses for new programs; annual meetings for clients, parents, volunteers and donors; membership meetings; reunions; and heritage societies are all social opportunities for people who show an interest in the mission of the service agency.

Reunions

Reunions are a means of keeping people involved even though they may have moved on in their lives. Educational organizations, especially private colleges, devote significant resources to keeping track of their graduates. They realize that, at some point, there is a good chance that many of the graduates will be willing to share their financial success with the institution that educated them. Churches are not as well organized in tracking past members, nor are human service agencies.

Reunions and reminiscing have a complicated pull. For those with pleasant associations, reunions are a positive, nostalgic and reinforcing experience. In some cases, people may have had painful experiences that helped them grow and do not really carry pleasant memories about the agency or institution. Nevertheless, curiosity about how everyone else is doing can win out. Making contact with the alumni can be as easy as putting an ad in the newspaper and the newsletter. Following is a sample message that is short but interesting and effective.

Do You Remember When
- The school was located on Sycamore Avenue?
- Dr. Mary Francis was the principal?
- Mrs. Hudmeyer taught fifth grade?

We haven't forgotten. And we haven't forgotten you and your classmates. Help us keep the memories alive. We need to hear from you. The Trinity Development office needs your current information in order to keep you up to date on our upcoming anniversary celebration (or capital campaign, national recognition, new program, or other major event).

The Annual Meeting

If the service agency is a membership organization, an annual meeting is usually a requirement. Members must elect board members and keep abreast of the agency's financial needs, its activities for the previous year, and its audited financial statements. Even if the agency is not a membership organization, an annual meeting for the entire constituency is a convenient way for the executive director and the board to present their reports and receive live feedback. It is also an excellent time to outline the needs of the coming year or years. Some organizations hold the annual meeting at the time when their financial audit has been completed. They distribute the audit or a simplified version to those people who request it.

The annual meeting has an additional advantage. It helps the agency maintain contact with its constituency. Those who are already involved with the organization enjoy hearing the latest official information and having the opportunity to offer some input. Those who have never been involved may learn enough about the agency and its programs to become involved in some capacity also.

The Annual Report

Some organizations find it helpful to have a nicely printed report that is a multi-purpose communication piece. It generally contains a letter from the executive director and/or the president of the board and highlights of the agency's recent accomplishments. To bring the work of the agency to the human level, it may also include pictures of clients in programs, outstanding volunteers and staff members. The report is usually mailed out judiciously because it is an expensive publication.

Nonetheless, some organizations send it to every donor, volunteer and family, in addition to the local newspaper and other media outlets.

Parent Associations and Caretaker Groups

Some service agencies hold separate meetings for the family members of the people it serves. While these meetings are important for informational purposes, they can also be used to attract other people to the work of the service agency. Some ways to do so include

- Inviting individuals who have been through the agency programs but have moved on with their lives
- Encouraging everyone to explore volunteer opportunities
- Urging people who are already involved to recruit new volunteers from the families of individuals who are currently being served
- Encouraging constituents to present volunteer and donor opportunities to persons in the community who are not connected to the agency in any way
- Presenting information on current programs and new initiatives.

A Capital Campaign

The need for capital for a building campaign can be the most cohesive force in building a loyal constituency. The realistic approach to goal setting, the resulting success that everyone feels when meeting goals, and the experience of working together can create a synergy that bonds both volunteers and staff to each other and the organization. Of course, the process is a difficult one as staff and volunteers work to generate the first 50 percent of the donations necessary for the ultimate success of the campaign. Then it can become somewhat tedious as workers continue to make contacts for the smaller gifts that make up the final 50 percent of the campaign goal. Nevertheless, experiencing those early successes and failures together can be a motivating force for the volunteers to stick with it to the end. In addition, their enthusiasm and sense of purpose can inspire others to become involved in the organization.

Recruiting Board Members or Trustees

Given the current financial climate, people in human service agencies need to examine the criteria for good board members. Once the organization establishes its mission statement along with short- and long-term goals, it should evaluate its current board members and their terms of office. Outlining the qualifications needed for new board members is also necessary since they will be charged with carrying the mission forward. Qualities might include wealth or influence, willingness to contribute, sufficient interest to ask probing questions about management and administration, and deep dedication to the organization's mission.[5] Board members for social service agencies should also be familiar with the issues relevant to the organization. That is why family members of clients and professionals in the field make good candidates for board positions.

In well-run organizations, term lengths for individual members of the board of directors are determined by the articles of incorporation. Some entities have terms with strict limits, that is, two, two-year terms or three, four-year terms. Other organizations do not limit the number of terms a board member may serve, and, in fact, some serve on the board for the rest of their active lives. The advantage of numerous terms for board members is that they have a clear understanding of the mission and challenges of the organization. The advantage of a defined number of years on the board is that new people come on with new perspectives on important policy-making functions, and the organization is revitalized.

The entire board and the executive director share the responsibility of seeking appropriate new board members. The nominating committee usually seeks suggestions from the board and the executive director for names of people who match the qualifications that the board has identified.

Attracting Quality Volunteers

Quality volunteers can make the difference between successful and mediocre fund-raising projects, so it is essential to learn which qualities characterize good volunteers. In his book, *Conducting a Successful Fundraising Program*, Kent E. Dove suggests that, in a specific fund-raising campaign, the best leaders are "excited and exciting" and they come mainly from within. Board members, service users, advisor groups and "other institutional family constituents" should lead the campaign.[6]

Furthermore, since the goal of the leaders is to raise money, they must be able to make significant gifts themselves as well as obtain them from other people they know. Therefore, Dove suggests that such high quality, fund-raising leaders fall into four main groups:

- Those who have inherited both wealth and its tradition of public service
- The newly rich and newly powerful
- The top professional managers of key corporations
- Respected and admired men and women of the community.[7]

People working in fund development commonly recommend that fund-raising leaders should be respected individuals with good community name recognition and effective leaders in their own fields. They should also demonstrate a strong belief in the goals of the organization, evidenced by their involvement in major gifts to the institution. These volunteer fund-raisers need to feel a passion for the cause they support since their enthusiasm will inspire others to give freely. The absence of this kind of leadership may signal that the organization is not ready to undertake a capital campaign.

> No one has ever become poor by giving.
>
> Anne Frank

Emphasizing Needs

Peter F. Drucker, perhaps the twentieth century's leading management thinker, recognized the elements necessary to a nonprofit's success. First, the organization must try to meet the management standards of the very best organizations. That means being accountable for performance and results, focusing their efforts on what they do best, and hiring out those functions that can be done better and more cheaply by a business.[8] No one knows better than the agency's leaders what needs to be accomplished. Clearly defining those needs and the actions necessary to meet them must be achieved before, during and after any fund-raising effort.

Expanding Organization Outreach

In order to develop its potential, the human service agency must attract and involve people interested in the organization's mission. Among other things, connecting with the right individuals will increase funding through private resources. To reach this goal, agencies can start by following some specific steps.

- Begin recruiting persons of affluence and influence to serve on a variety of committees. Educate them about your mission and involve them in the organization's activities.
- Expand the use of volunteers in your fund-raising efforts, which can include:
  1. The annual appeal to increase your current financial goal
  2. Special events to raise money for current needs or capital
  3. Donor clubs to encourage increased levels of giving
  4. A "legacy society" to focus on a planned giving program
  5. A planned giving council of professionals.
- Start a support foundation for the existing operating entity whose purpose is to promote stewardship and perhaps act as the holding company for capital assets.
- Raise the visibility of the organization.
- Create an alumni association of clients and families.
- Develop a formal program to recognize donors and volunteers.

The following chapters develop each of these areas in greater depth.

3

BARRIERS TO SUCCESSFUL FUND RAISING

Most of the fund-raising articles and successes that are reported in magazines and books stem from campaigns run by colleges, universities, hospitals, and other large, highly visible charities. They tend to be institutions in major metropolitan areas or national organizations with local offices and services. By contrast, many human service agencies lack the advantages of the larger nonprofits, so they experience some significant difficulties in obtaining the resources necessary to provide services to people who need them.

Many human service agencies serve people with disabilities–both persons born with severe limitations and those who suffer disabilities caused by the environment, accidents or addictions. Unfortunately, this is a relatively significant portion of the population. Statistics show that the incidence of severe, disabling conditions for persons from birth to age 21 ranges from one to seven percent (not including learning disabilities).[1] In addition, severe disability for persons 65 and older is much higher sim-

> No person was
> ever honored
> for what he received.
> Honor has been
> the reward
> for what he gave.
>
> Calvin Coolidge

ply because mild problems evolve into greater challenges as aging begins to play a part.

Traditional Government Funding

Traditionally, services to people with disabilities have been funded by the government. Socially responsible citizens have recognized that these individuals need an economic safety net and special services to be able to develop to their maximum potential. In the past century in particular, that has translated into government-supported programs operated by local organizations. The majority of the financial backing for the services has come from state governments, with fairly significant matching funds from the federal government through Medicaid.

Customarily, the philanthropic community has supported the concept that this is the role of government and has not wanted to supplant that responsibility. However, now that most state governments are experiencing record-breaking deficits, full government funding of those programs is definitely at risk. The economic climate has, unfortunately, also impacted donations to the United Way, an organization that has provided a large portion of the local, voluntary funding.[2]

> We are all handicapped in one way or another. Sometimes, it can be seen on the outside; sometimes it is on the inside.
>
> Mother Teresa

Modest Alumni Contributions

Some groups of potential donors achieve success in much larger numbers than individuals who have been served by local human service agencies. Typically, these include the alumni of high visibility organizations such as colleges, universities and hospitals, and the constituencies that stem from their alumni associations. Some agencies serve extremely vulnerable populations who often face multiple and complex challenges. Success for them ranges from being able to become at least partly self-sufficient in daily living skills to becoming independent and having the ability to work, earn a living and spend a large portion of their time controlling their own futures and their own activities.

Financial stability is certainly a problem for persons with disabilities. The 2000 U.S. Census indicates that for all persons who are not high school graduates, the mean annual earnings are 16,053 dollars versus 43,782 dollars for someone with a bachelor's degree and 95,488 dollars for individuals with a professional degree. The upper ranges of attainment are simply not a possibility for many people who have significant disabilities.[3]

In addition to the individuals' financial challenges, the families of children born with disabilities often have unusually high expenses. As a result, they may never develop the kind of wealth that enables them to make large, charitable gifts to any organizations. Certainly, wealthy and powerful individuals also have family members with disabilities, but the truly wealthy families are few. The U.S. Census data for 2000 indicates that out of approximately 106.9 million males of all races, only 6.1 million had earned incomes of over 100,000 dollars a year. The same data indicates that out of about 114.7 million females, only 1.6 million had earned incomes over 100,000 dollars a year.[4]

Individuals served by human service agencies who do not have multiple and complex challenges, such as people affected by addictions, abuse, homelessness and poverty, also have less chance of being able to give financial aid because their opportunities for success are more limited. Certainly, there are a number of cases where overcoming multiple obstacles simply intensifies the desire to achieve financial success, but those are more likely exceptions.

Composition of Human Service Agency Boards

For a smoothly run organization, a nonprofit board needs an optimal mix of persons representing various elements. Typically, service agencies strive for between 20 and 30 percent participation from the family members and individuals who have personally experienced the problems addressed by the agency. Another 20 percent might be professionals in the social service field–people who have valuable knowledge about the mission of the organization but do not have the benefit of upper-range financial resources. That leaves about one half of the board positions open for people who have other helpful skills. For instance, a person who can make large contributions or who knows individuals with great resources can be an effective fund-raiser.

Facing Various Decreases in Contributions

Giving USA, quoted in the June 26, 2003, edition of *The Chronicle of Philanthropy*, issued a statement noting that while charitable giving was up for 2002 over 2001, it did not keep pace with inflation. The largest drop in giving was to social service groups. It further stated that "charities providing human services received $18.7 billion, or 7.7 percent, of the Giving USA total. Social service groups suffered the largest drop in contributions from 2001, falling 11.3 percent after accounting for inflation."[5] These decreases have an inevitable, detrimental effect on human service agencies. Gary Cardaronella, a professional fund-raiser and member of the Giving USA Editorial Review Board, states that agencies serving the needy "are often small organizations that have not developed really strong constituents. What I suspect is that many of these organizations get lots of support from lots of different people. But often there are not really, really large gifts from really wealthy people. So they are not able to weather economic downturns."[6]

Prejudices Against Fund Raising

Many people feel inhibited about asking for money to help worthy causes because they associate it with begging. Sometimes, they are embarrassed to ask; other times they do not know what to say; and still other times, they wonder, "Why should people give because I asked? I'm no one special." Professionals in human services also often believe that the government should provide full services for people who are experiencing severe difficulties. They are convinced that it is inappropriate to ask for money. Their belief is that it reinforces the concept of being unfortunate and deserving of pity, a negative element in the life of a person with complex challenges. Adopting this attitude undermines his dignity and personal worth.

However, human service professionals need to understand that asking others to help in whatever way they can—including giving money—is an opportunity that many donors appreciate. They would like to help a disadvantaged person in some way, but are unable to because their talents do not lie in that area. Offering them a method of helping can be a win-win situation for both the giver and the donee. Why not let concerned individuals experience the satisfaction of knowing that they are helping others?

Community Prejudices Against "Outsiders"

Because of the system used in many states for referring people to appropriate organizations for care, the agency serving the person is often not in the community where the individual and his family live. This is partly because the service delivery system is designed to prevent duplication of services. Sometimes, so few individuals experience a certain disability or combination of disabilities that services need to be centralized elsewhere. Prior to the 1980s, individuals with developmental disabilities and mental illness were frequently institutionalized far from their families.

Fortunately, the climate has changed dramatically since then. However, when priorities in funding shifted and methods for dealing with disabilities first began to change, people in residential facilities were moved from one place to another simply because there was a room available. Where they lived was given little consideration.

Since the persons receiving services are often seen as "outsiders," people in a community will frequently resist supporting those services even though they are willing to aid residents of their own area. This attitude is prevalent in suburban communities that may regularly receive a significant number of persons with complex needs from a major city nearby. But, the argument has been used by people in rural communities who do not want to serve those from a town ten miles away, or by residents on the north side of a major city who do not wish to provide care for persons from the south side of the same city. Of course, the situation is exacerbated when people who have mental illness and/or addiction issues wander into a facility for services or are jailed for some reason and are unable to identify themselves properly.

> If you want happiness for a lifetime, help somebody.
>
> Chinese proverb

Reminding community members that we are a very mobile society may help residents to think differently. For example, they need to consider questions like, "Were you born in this community?" "Do all your relatives live in the same town?" "Do all your children live in the area where you were born and grew up?" Answers to these questions generally force people to realize that few in the community have lived there all their lives.

Fear of People with Complex Challenges

Many individuals are willing to make financial contributions to help people with complex challenges as long as the facility where services are provided is located at some distance from their homes. This results from a variety of fears. Some are afraid that they or a member of their family may suffer violence because of a client's behavioral issues. Others worry that their children will be affected negatively or that property value will plummet should a service agency open in the neighborhood. Still others fear that customers will avoid patronizing local businesses or that new businesses will not move to the area.

As leaders of these organizations know, there are fewer problems if the individuals being served have mental retardation rather than mental illness coupled with aggression, a history of violence or prison time. Needless to say, most agencies will not accept persons who are dangerous to themselves or others, though occasional episodes of inappropriate and violent behavior may occur.

Ironically, the truth is that inappropriate and violent behaviors occur with regularity in the "normal" population, creating situations that can frighten people with disabilities. For example, the son of a friend of mine has schizophrenia and lives in a carefully maintained, well-organized group home. One evening, he called 911 because the neighbors, a husband and wife, were having a loud, nasty fight. He was afraid that there might be a violent episode between them. Obviously, fear of harm is not the sole purview of persons in the general population.

4

RAISING THE VISIBILITY OF THE AGENCY

People—whether potential volunteers or donors—are interested in helping a human service agency if they know the organization, the type of people it serves, what it does, and how community members could support the cause. It must, therefore, communicate its presence in a variety of ways.

This presents a catch 22. If the agency wants companies to hire its clients, then administrators need to communicate with the decision makers. If the agency wants to raise money for unmet needs, then the governing body must be willing to communicate how money is spent and which programs are not adequately funded.

In order to make those essential connections with the community and business, agency staff and administrators must learn about community education programs. Following are some communication methods that may be employed.

A Regular Newsletter

The newsletter should cover:

- New programs
- Individual successes
- Future plans
- Upcoming events
- Recognition of volunteers and donors
- News about the staff
- Unmet needs
- Voluntary giving opportunities
- Volunteer opportunities
- A place and person to call or write for more information

Regular Open Houses

Open houses are an opportunity for the service agency to show the media and potential donors, volunteers and board members how its programs and initiatives work and what it is accomplishing for the people it serves. There is no substitute for firsthand information–seeing, hearing, smelling, touching and tasting. The visitor who samples the good food clients eat, who hears the reassuring voice of a direct care worker, or who sees a nurse's gentle touch is in an excellent position to describe to others the work being done. And, she is less likely to ignore or forget the human needs that must be met.

Regular Press Releases

Press releases should be delivered to the media sources such as newspapers, radio, television and community news Web sites. Agency public relations personnel should follow up news releases with telephone calls to editors and specific writers to prompt them to do a story on agency concerns, accomplishments, events and needs. Topics that might be covered include:

- Community problems the agency is trying to address
- New programs
- Innovations
- Client successes
- Program successes
- Staff accomplishments and honors
- Volunteer accomplishments
- Upcoming open houses or annual meetings
- New board members
- Individual board member profiles
- Grants from the government and other funding sources
- Unmet needs
- Gifts from local entities
- An upcoming event, noting leaders, type and location of event, ticket price and purpose of fund-raiser

- An event follow-up, including photos of attendees, detailed description of the event, winners of contests and amount of money raised
- Annual campaign, noting participants, purpose and subject matter, time, progress reports and final reports
- Capital campaigns, noting participants, purpose, type of campaign, time and progress reports, final reports, recognition of participants and press parties for committee members
- Volunteer opportunities, noting opportunties available, job descriptions and qualifications, and times volunteers are needed
- Volunteer recognition
- Legislative issues affecting the organization
- Celebrity promoters (i.e., state or United States senators, representatives, governors, mayors, corporate or foundation presidents, union leaders, movie stars, athletes), noting time and purpose of visit.

Features for Other Publications

Years ago, it would have been unthinkable to have the organization write a story about some aspect of the organization's activities and have a newspaper publish it. Now, because newspapers have fewer full-time reporters and often hire freelancers ("stringers") to write feature stories, they are more open to printing a story written by a competent writer within the service agency. It is best for the official spokesperson to write the story and have it published in its entirety, since newspaper reporters are often rushed or do not understand the nuances of the subject matter.

A recent example of inaccurate reporting occurred when Barbara McGoldrick was being interviewed about an innovative idea she was spearheading. It involved the combined efforts of a local mental health advocacy agency, a direct service provider, and a group of parents of young adults with mental illness. This coalition was working to provide for the future care of persons with severe disabilities without jeopardizing their Social Security and Medicare benefits. The plan was to create a special needs trust and have one set of parents fund it with enough money to make a down payment on a nice but ordinary, four-bedroom house. In addition, a local bank would provide the mortgage. Housing vouchers from the U.S. Department of Housing and Urban Development for the four individuals who would live in the house would cover the cost of a direct service provider to handle maintenance, staffing and other essentials of their care. The adult child of the family (the primary beneficiary of the special needs trust) would live with three roommates with compatible personalities and needs. The parents of this young adult could relax, knowing that their child had a home, companions and care even after their death. They were also hoping to acquire a second home using the same strategy.

Unfortunately, the interviewing reporter totally missed the point of the plan and stated in the newspaper story that when the homes were acquired, they would be turned over to the state. That was definitely not the case. The state would be providing funding for transportation, programming and needed staffing but would never own the homes. All of the people involved in the plan began a great flurry of phone calls because they were concerned that details of the program had been changed. However, the reporter had simply misunderstood the information provided.

> Think of giving
> not as a duty
> but as a privilege.
>
> John D. Rockefeller, Jr.

Stories written about the agency can also be used as enclosures in letters to individuals and groups, legitimizing its work and mission.

Damage Control in the Press

Just as it is a pleasure to announce good news, it is a challenge to deal with bad news. Loss of funding is certainly bad, but the worst news involves occasions when someone at an agency facility is badly injured, a building burns down, someone is suing the organization, a client commits suicide, or abuse by either an employee or client is discovered. In these cases, damage control is the objective.

Negative news always receives much higher priority and coverage from the media than good news. It is critical that there be a staff member designated as spokesperson who is trained to deal with such scenarios. Since there are legal ramifications as well as public relations issues, it is also critical that other staff members know they are not to speak to the media unless the administration gives its approval. People can easily be misquoted or make offhand remarks during a conversation and cause the organization to incur further liability.

Books Promoting the Agency

Books can also be used as promotional tools for the service agency. Agency staff or constituency may include writers and/or photographers willing to produce a book on the agency, its work and the people it serves.

An excellent example of a book promoting an agency mission is *Images from Within: Portraits of People Confronting Mental Illness* by Alisa Hauser and Marc Hauser. Alisa, a local social rehabilitation counselor and freelance writer, was inspired to write a story about the people with mental illness who were served by Trinity Services, Inc. in Lockport, Illinois. She had seen the controversy caused by merchants who objected to having mentally ill people going in and out of Trinity buildings. They insisted that customers were reluctant to come into their stores because they felt threatened by the Trinity clients. In an effort to combat this attitude, Alisa decided to write a book. She presented each individual with mental illness as a person with a unique story. She also convinced her second cousin Marc, an award-winning photographer, to do a portrait of each person to accompany the appropriate vignettes.

Trinity paid to have the book published and uses it in many ways to help create understanding about the ways people deal with their own mental illness. They are people like anyone else, living in communities, holding down jobs or working toward employment. And, they are trying to triumph over their illness.

Creating and Using Marketing Materials

Professionally prepared marketing materials are essential to communicating what the agency does and whom it serves. These are not limited to, but should include, the following:

General Brochures

General brochures should be threefold, printed on both sides and sized to fit in ordinary business envelopes. The agency mission, a brief summary of its programs, at least one or two pictures, and attractive graphic design make the brochure both informative and appealing. Information must be updated regularly to reflect any changes in the agency's activities. The main address, telephone and fax numbers should also be featured prominently along with the Web site if there is one.

Program Fact Sheets

The only thing certain in life is that things will change. Fact sheets offer a cost effective method of displaying and distributing program information on individual sheets. When changes occur, the sheet for the appropriate program can be updated, saving the organization a good deal of money. Keeping fact sheets current is essential. Otherwise, it is possible to distribute information about programs that no longer exist, fail to promote a new program that needs publicity, or fail to respond appropriately to changes in target client populations.

One example of an excellent informational packet is the one used by Trinity Services, Inc. This human service agency serves approximately 1,300 people in over 100 different locations scattered throughout five densely populated counties in northern Illinois, and Reno and Carson City, Nevada. They developed a series of program descriptions on individual sheets of paper in graduated sizes that are placed neatly in a handsome green folder, measuring twelve by nine inches. The title of the program appears in bold-face type on the left-hand side of each fact sheet. The right side of the folder contains more specific information for the targeted audience. These might include reprinted newspaper articles, the most recent audit, a position paper on new legislation or other pertinent materials.

While printed materials represent an expensive part of the communication process, they are essential. It is virtually impossible for agency leaders and staff to communicate in person or by telephone all of the necessary information a potential client, donor, employee or media contact person needs. Also, printed materials offer the agency a tremendous opportunity to communicate their mission and values through carefully planned specifics (language) and intangibles (color, shape, lettering, etc.). Standard-sized materials are usually less costly to produce because printers do not have to charge an extra fee for sizing. The cost of mailing standard-sized envelopes is also lower.

Often, completing desktop publishing in house can save money. It may be suitable for a small agency in a small community, as long as a technically competent individual prepares the material. Desktop publishing can also be used economically by an agency of any size if informational pieces are intended for a limited number of people or for personalized letters.

Although in-house printing is very tempting, the high cost of ink often defeats the assumed savings when volume becomes an issue. Furthermore, it should never be used for pieces that are expected to last for a year and will be mailed to several thousand people. These informational materials should be produced professionally so they proclaim: "We are excellent at what we do, and we believe in professional quality," not "We did this ourselves with loving hands at home."

> Let us not hesitate to encourage each other to be grateful for the gifts we have received.
>
> Jean Vanier

Fact sheets promoting the organization's work often last a long time in the hands of people who care about the agency. The public relations department should use the services of a graphic designer who understands the agency's purpose and provides design choices that capture the essence of the agency's mission. Lasting images should be given careful consideration since they say a lot about the agency's culture and reputation.

Printed materials can also offer an outstanding opportunity to interact with the business community. For example, agency staff may find a printer who is willing to print an entire project at cost in exchange for recognition of their contribution on the literature. Acknowledgements might include "Printing donated by ABC Company," "Paper donated by XYZ Company," or "Printing underwritten by GHI Company."

Audio-Visual Productions

The old saying that a picture is worth a thousand words is especially true when an agency is promoting its work and the people it serves. High quality audio-visuals are the next best thing to having a potential donor tour the organization's facilities. All of the principles of projecting a quality image in print apply to preparing a video, compact disk (CD) or digital video disk (DVD). The advantage, of couse, is that videos, CD's and DVD's can be both seen and heard.

While the organization must provide the content, the public relations department should hire professionals to shape the final product in order to ensure a high quality production. A professional announcer should narrate the presentation. A local television or radio announcer might be willing to narrate the video presentation, which could also be produced as an audiotape, CD and/or DVD. A talented writer and an editor acquainted with film production should script the voice-over and integrate it with small sound bites from people in the film. Chances are very high that a local community college has a program for audio-visual production and would be willing to make its facilities available to produce the program if a professional cannot be found. In addition, students who have talent in this arena can organize a team to work on the project. They would not only benefit from the experience but could also keep a copy of the "documentary" they produced to include in their portfolios.

The completed audio-visual piece, along with a brochure or fact sheets, can be handed out to concerned community members and organizations. It can also provide the basis for a number of public presentations. (See "Speakers on Call" and "Using Volunteers as Ambassadors.") In addition, a local television or radio station might be willing to run the finished product as a public service.

Agency Web Sites

Given the proliferation of people available to design Web sites, it is a relatively easy process to find a person or a company to design an agency Web site. If the service agency wishes to save money, staff members or constituents may be asked to refer a professional in the field who can do the majority of the work at no cost. In return, the professional could display an ad on the agency Web site, noting that this site is an example of her work. The quality of the site is good publicity for both the service agency and the designer.

Creating content for a Web site is just as labor intensive as preparing the words and images for a brochure. Likewise, maintaining the site with current information is just as important as keeping brochure information up to date. Fortunately, much of the same material can appear in both. The main difference is that both copy and images are easier to change on a Web site. Unless the agency has an in-house Web site technician, it must pay a modest fee to keep the site current. Keeping a site on the Web also entails an ongoing charge.

Since the agency Web site's purpose is to provide information to the public, it should be easy to use, aimed at the general public and connected to browsers that are the most popular. Agency staff and the designer should keep in mind that they are trying to get the attention of people who are looking for information, though an interesting site will also attract the notice of a person who is simply "surfing" the Web. Therefore, an eye-catching design is important. Another key is having links to various search engines. This ensures that the service agency appears in the listings when a visitor enters the organization name, or service description and geographic location.

One enormous advantage of a Web page is that it can provide an up-to-date listing of events, where tickets are sold and contributions are made. A contract with a Web service provider can give the agency access to an online payment service. However, many people are still unwilling to use their credit cards online. For example, the San Jose Dioceses in California found that only a few people make reservations and pay for monthly meetings online using their credit cards. The majority preferred to make the reservations online and then fax credit card numbers for payment purposes. Chances are, the agency will face similar reluctance even if it provides Web site visitors with security assurances. It is wise to offer the agency fax number for the donor's use. Ticket buyers or donors should always have the option of sending a check or money order through the mail unless a time-sensitive Internet promotion is being used, such as last-minute tickets to an event or raffle.

Speakers on Call

Many community organizations are looking for polished presentations about various aspects of community life. A speaker's bureau, often called "Speakers on Call" or a similar name, provides an opportunity for the service agency to make its programs and successes known to a number of audiences. Ideally, a staff member should be the designated speaker. Every organization has individuals who can communicate effectively with audiences. Often, it is the executive director or another staff member. Sometimes, it is a parent, family member or even the clients themselves. The speaker must be articulate, interesting and able to answer questions from the audience accurately. As soon as the speaker starts presenting with competence, word of mouth will bring more and more requests. Once speaking engagements become more numerous, it is possible to expand the agency speaker's bureau to other staff members, board members and volunteers.

Staff members can generate openings for these presentations by sending a letter that outlines the types of programs the agency can present to all local clubs and civic organizations. Presentations should include stories of persons served by the agency. Some clients may agree to share their achievements with others. This allows the speaker to use pictures, first names and heart-warming accounts of success. Similarly, it is appropriate to include stories of ongoing challenges as long as the client and family have consented. Pity has no place in these presentations. They are meant to help change social attitudes and put into perspective some of the challenges that audience members face. An overly hectic work schedule, for example, pales in comparison to the inability to hold down a job at all.

The presentations will most likely bring contributions to the agency. Organizations almost always give speakers an honorarium, which translates into a contribution. When the needs of the organization are fully communicated and audiences connect with the people and their needs, the club or association will often follow up with still another contribution from its own general fund. Some clubs like to photograph the presentation of a check to the speaker so it can be published in their newsletter or even in the newspaper. This publicity offers another opportunity for service agency visibility.

One very effective public program was the Ray Graham Association Singers, all of whom were persons with a variety of disabilities. The choral group, led by a talented musical director, had performed not only in their own community, but statewide and nationally. They said more through their musical performance than any speaker could. Their intent, shining faces accompanied by unified, beautiful tones gave audiences a unique and memorable experience.

Volunteers as Speakers

Assuming that the agency has printed materials and possibly an audio-visual presentation, the public relations department can broaden the scope of the community education/fund-raising program by employing volunteers as representatives. A client, parent or family member who gives a third party endorsement is especially valuable to the agency. A board member who is also a volunteer has a different value as a presenter because she knows many of the policy issues and funding needs of the organization. DuPage Easter Seal, for example, had a number of board members who were as effective with certain audiences as the executive director was with others.

> Wherever there is a human being, there is an opportunity for kindness.
>
> Seneca

The delicate part about using volunteers is that some people are not very good public speakers. They should be allowed to show an audio-visual presentation only when it is preceded and concluded by a prepared script. This will maintain the quality public relations opportunity that benefits the service agency. On the other hand, when the volunteers are good public speakers, they are fabulous ambassadors who often do better without sticking to a script.

If the agency staff continually educates volunteers about what the organization does and what it needs, they can all be volunteer ambassadors. For instance, they can help to identify employment opportunities for clients by opening the door to employers they know personally. They can also encourage families who have members that would benefit from agency services. In addition, the volunteers can help work on important legislative issues, present financial needs to a broader audience, and introduce agency personnel to people who have money and might be willing to contribute to a deserving cause.

5

FUND-RAISING STRATEGIES

Educating people about the agency's services and needs enables an organization to find new donors and new volunteers. It is a never-ending process that is often difficult and always time-consuming. Fortunately, education and fund raising occur simultaneously in most cases, and a wide variety of means are available for organizations to consider. First, volunteers, administrators and staff should determine how many volunteer fund-raising activities they can and should organize in the course of a year. Many of them are synergistic and do not take away from each other. Participants become more aware and more involved while also attracting new people into agency fund-raising efforts.

> Any task of love is
> a task of peace,
> no matter
> how insignificant
> it may seem.
>
> Mother Teresa

Direct Mailings versus Volunteer-led Mailings

Organizations use three main strategies for mailings. One involves writing to people who are already familiar with the agency's services and have supported them in the past. The agency achieves some degree of cost effectiveness with this strategy because the donors are renewals who are already acquainted with the agency's mission and work. One agency in Illinois raises several thousand dollars through mass mailings to its list of 11,000 persons. The letter is signed by the volunteer, board chair and perhaps the executive director as well.

The second starts with naming a campaign chairperson, who then recruits volunteers who are willing to put personal notes into mailings that will reach existing and potential donors with whom they are acquainted. This strategy is usually a component of the agency's annual fund-raising campaign or a capital campaign, and usually brings the greatest return because it is personalized and volunteer driven.

The third strategy is a mailing to cold prospects, usually identified from lists provided by a mailing list service. While these mailings might also go to existing donors, the main goal is to recruit new donors with no previous ties to the agency. Letters are not personalized by volunteers, though the board chairperson usually signs each of them. (See Chapter 6: Maintaining a Database.)

The organization's fund-raising committee must recognize, however, that direct mailings are not as effective as some other methods. James M. Greenfield, senior associate vice president of The Alford Group, estimates that up to 90 percent of all appeal letters are thrown away unopened. And, of those who open appeal letters, only ten percent will reply with a donation.[1] *That's a one percent response!*

When mailings are sent, Greenfield suggests writing personal letters that get the readers' attention. It is also essential to describe the need that exists in the community. In addition, letters should emphasize the organization's ability to provide answers to the problem, and invite the reader to be part of the solution.

Restrictions on direct mail appeals may apply to some community agencies in certain areas if they receive funds from the United Way. The best approach in these cases is to include a formal letter composed by the chairperson of either the annual campaign or the volunteer board, and possibly signed by the executive director. Furthermore, volunteers should mail at least some letters to their friends. Letters should include a hand-addressed envelope and a note at the top of the letter, or on a separate card, asking the acquaintance to support this deserving cause. Indeed, people do respond better to friends, and a hand-addressed envelope is opened much more readily than one that is obviously a mass mailing.

Unfortunately, using direct mail to acquire donors for the first time is a very expensive proposition. On average, it costs an organization $1.25 to $1.50 to raise just one dollar through first time acquisition mailings (that is, mailings to people not associated in any way with the service agency).[2] Even with carefully selected mailing lists and expert advice on designing and mailing the letter, it does not make good economic sense for most community agencies to spend that kind of money to recruit new donors.

On the other hand, an annual campaign, led by a volunteer chairperson and the volunteers he recruits, can be very cost effective. As long as the chairperson and volunteers are a blend of veterans and new recruits, the agency is assured of a new batch of potential donors each year. Current volunteers provide the necessary continuity and can write personal notes, reaching the same people they have in the past. For their part, the new volunteers can write to their friends, asking for donations and connecting the organization to a whole new pool of potential donors. Hopefully, when these donors receive regular newsletters and communiques about what the organization is doing, they will respond positively even if the volunteer who originally approached them is no longer actively involved. The original personal contact is key.

Maintaining contact and convincing potential donors of the value of their contribution is also key. The well-organized charity tracks volunteer/donor correlation in its donor files. Knowing which volunteer note elicited a contribution during one campaign will enable the chairperson to recruit the right volunteer to write a note the following year, thus maximizing renewals.

Special Events

Another common fund-raising strategy is to produce several special events throughout the year. Events are an extremely effective way to achieve volunteer involvement because they can be organized by volunteers with staff supervision and assistance. They allow volunteers to put their creativity and their hands to work for the cause in a way that is usually not possible in the organization's day-to-day programming. Volunteers become excited about an event when it reflects their interests and talents.

A main advantage of special events is that they offer excellent opportunities to attract new supporters and educate the broader community about the work of the organization. While the annual fund-raising appeal can seem like difficult work, events raise money while providing a pleasant experience for both the people who work on it and the participants.

Revenue sources for a special event usually start with ticket sales, ad programs, sponsorships and in-kind gifts. The event then elicits funds through silent auctions, live auctions, raffle ticket sales, in-kind gifts or any combination of these four activities.

The costs usually include expenses related to printing the invitations, tickets and programs; postage; food and beverages; decorations; favors; entertainment; parking assistance or some form of transportation; and facility rental. There is great variation in the cost of special events. For example, it may be held in a venue designed for special events, in the organization's own facility, in a sponsor's facility, or in a new or unusual location. The food may be hors d'oeuvres or a lavish sit-down meal. In all cases, the direct cost of the benefit should never exceed 50 percent of the money raised (excluding staff time).

Special events that work well for community organizations include

- Art shows
- Antique shows
- Auto shows
- Fashion shows
- Concerts
- Opening nights
- Dining with a celebrity
- Luncheons or dinners with auction items and drawings
- In-home parties
- Garden walks
- House walks
- Raffles
- Sports contests
- Sporting events

The volunteers' enthusiasm often drives the selection of special events. After all, they are the ones who must be committed to the event in order to make it successful. Following are some key elements that are necessary for having successful fund-raising events.

Art Shows

Art shows can be held at local art galleries or other facilities. Owners or managers of galleries want to feature their wares and are often willing to donate a percentage of any sale to the charity. If the show is held at a another facility, such as a performing arts center or an upscale cafe, organizers can raise money by selling tickets and charging participating artists a fee to exhibit their pieces, or the artists can donate a percentage of their sale. The artists might be clients of the service agency, residents of the community, or professionals who are invited to come to town for the occasion.

Prize drawings during the event offer the organizers an opportunity to collect each attendee's name, address and telephone number. It is a wonderful way to acquire new contacts for the agency's mailing list. A thank you note to those who attended or worked on the event is another, more formal method of "friend raising."

> The more you give,
> the more
> you will receive,
> because you will keep
> the abundance
> of the universe
> circulating in your life.
>
> Deepak Chopra

Art shows can be very enjoyable affairs. One very lovely art show was held on the grounds of the Cantigny Museum in Wheaton, Illinois. It ran for three days and featured artists from all over the country, who came by invitation. The show was also juried. Attendees paid a modest admission fee, though the opening night was more expensive since the evening's attractions included wine, soft drinks and delicious hors d'oeuvres.

Another art show was held at an indoor arena rather than a gallery. The ticket price for the opening night was 75 dollars since the evening featured a juried art show, drinks and a variety of foods. Admission for the next two days was five dollars. This plan ensured a wide audience for the artists' works as well as a special event for individuals who had the means and the desire to attend.

Antique Shows

Antique shows have wide appeal in certain communities. Volunteers who are interested in antiques can host a show by inviting antique dealers to exhibit their wares.

The organization can collect funds by asking the dealers to pay a fee to exhibit. Or, they can join forces with an existing antique show. For the latter, agency volunteers should request to have the exhibiting dealers included in the opening night. Then, they can pursue the options of charging for admission and serving food. Refreshments can include anything from hor d'oeuvres to a box supper to a sit-down dinner, if space permits. The committee should also decide whether the sit-down dinner would be more beneficial than a formal or an informal affair.

A white elephant table with donated objects provides another way to raise money if the antique show organizers and exhibitors are agreeable. An expert appraiser on site is still another appealing attraction. He can provide a genuine appraisal of favorite inherited and acquired antiques that attendees bring. The main objective is to host an event that attracts people and offers the agency an opportunity to introduce its cause to a wider audience.

Auto Shows

Classic car collectors are always happy to bring their prize possessions to a show. In fact, some classic car clubs will help make the arrangements, reducing the work load on agency volunteers. Outdoor space is the easiest to acquire. Occasionally, a shopping center will permit the use of its interior space or a section of the parking lot for such a show. Volunteers can also approach park districts, festivals, restaurants, automotive businesses or any other organization that has open space for use. The show production committee can organize a program, sell tickets, and set up a tent to sell or serve food and beverages. The main drawback to any outdoor event, of course, is the unpredictability of the weather.

New car shows offer another fund-raising option. An auto dealer with a special interest in the service agency may be willing to host an auto show of new models. Sometimes, the dealer will even underwrite the costs for food and beverages.

One of the best fund-raisers in the Chicago area is the Chicago Auto Show, held at the McCormick Place Convention Center. The show runs for four or five days and attracts thousands of people. The auto dealers association chooses a group of charities that will benefit from the opening night event, which is often a black tie occasion. Each charity receives a certain number of tickets to sell, and they all share in the proceeds–usually 50,000 dollars or more. The larger the number of tickets sold by each charity, the higher the percentage of the proceeds they receive.

Fashion Shows

Fashion shows are also good fund-raisers, and there are a couple of ways to organize them. First, agency volunteers can ask a major retailer that regularly holds fashion shows for their own sales and promotional benefit to allow the agency to be the beneficiary of one show. Sometimes, store managers will want to produce the event in the store and will stage the entire show, using professional models. The organization's only commitment would be the sale of a specific number of tickets. Usually, the store will also pay for refreshments in order to control the menu, the choice of caterer and other elements of the show. One drawback that the volunteer committee needs to consider is that space is often limited and only a relatively small number of people can attend.

This type of fashion show is generally staged by retailers with high end merchandise and marketing budgets that allow for such exposure. The producers expect the organization to attract the type of people who can afford their clothes. If the planning committee does its part effectively, the entire ticket revenue will most likely go to the charity.

In another approach to the fashion show, the service agency finds a facility, erects a runway, creates the lighting, selects the store or stores that will be showing, plans the menu and uses amateur models from its own constituency. This can be equally–if not more–effective when the goal is to have a large number of attendees (about 300). A banquet facility works well because lunch and a fashion show make a nice combination. The constituent models–men and women–often help bring in more ticket sales than professional models since they invite their friends to support the cause. Children's fashions with child models from the committee constituency always bring oohs and aahs.

DuPage (Illinois) Easter Seals hosts an annual fashion show, using a professional coordinator to arrange the order of the fashions and provide commentary.

Among the models are children who have used Easter Seal services. The show includes a silent auction, raffle and ad program book that all generate more revenue. Their raffle technique is very effective. Organizers invite a number of handsome, outgoing young men dressed in tuxedos to walk around and sell raffle tickets to the mostly female audience. Attention to such details can make a fashion show an extremely lucrative fund-raiser.

Concerts

Buying a block of discounted tickets to a well-organized concert is one more way of raising money. Usually, there are two or more levels of ticket sales. The agency can make a reasonable amount from the basic ticket sales but charge a larger amount for better seats. If the agency volunteers can book a private reception with the headline performers after the concert, they can charge even more for good seats and tickets to the reception. Prices might range from 25 dollars for a basic ticket, 50 dollars for a good seat, and 75 dollars for an even better seat, to 100 dollars for the best seat. Larger donors might pay 150 dollars for the best seat and access to the reception. Prices should be structured to cover the cost of the tickets and reception with at least a 50 percent profit. Ancillary revenue sources might include an advertising program, raffle tickets or other items. Performers may be willing to share revenue from sales of autographed photos, music CDs or other similar items.

The service agency may also opt to book the concert itself and sell all the tickets. However, that can be a big risk, depending on the size of the organization and its ability to sell tickets.

Opening Nights

In the quest for new and unusual events to attract untapped supporters and keep long-standing supporters from being bored with repetitious events, opening nights provide some unique opportunities. Restaurants, movies, theatrical productions and stores all offer possible opening benefits for the service agency.

Restaurants

When new restaurants open, the owners want some special publicity while they train their staff to provide high quality food and service. With that in mind, fundraising committee members can be on the lookout for announcements of restaurant openings in the community. After locating a new restaurant, a volunteer can make a strategic telephone call to the owner or management, offering to help get attention via an opening night benefit.

The emphasis of the event would be, of course, on the food, drinks and ambiance. Volunteers may find that a beverage wholesaler, wine company or liquor distributor wants to promote a special brand and would be willing to offer specific beverages for free. Also, the restaurant or its meat vendor might offer the food at a deep discount—or even free. In exchange, they gain access to a crowd of patrons who like to try things first and are willing to buy tickets that benefit a respected, charitable organization.

> The intention behind your giving should always be to create happiness for the giver and receiver.
>
> Deepak Chopra

Another feature that tends to attract an audience is a local dignitary or celebrity at the event. As always, the "who's who" element interests local media and friends of those who attend. If all goes well, the experience is a positive one for both the restaurant management and all other participants.

Shopping Centers and Individual Stores

When a new retail store is coming to town, the owners and manager may have already budgeted for a special opening event. It is worthwhile to get in touch with the business headquarters to see if management would like to host the event as a benefit for the service agency. The advantage of this type of event is that expenses are minimized because the retailer is already planning a promotional celebration. The agency is simply helping to introduce the store (or shopping center) to the community by selling tickets to the opening and the merchandise preview. Private, after-hour shopping events are yet another alternative for volunteers to pursue with the owners of the shopping center or the lead stores.

Movies

In this era of mega movie complexes, a movie opening can be rather complicated to run as a special fund-raiser. But, if a board member, agency staff person or key supporter knows someone in the theater management, something special is possible.

The chosen contact can approach the manager or owner for permission to host the event on the night when a major movie is released. If the management is agreeable, the fund-raising committee can negotiate a block of tickets at a reduced price to be sold by volunteers and friends.

Committee members might also consider organizing a champagne or wine reception in the lobby of the theater. In a major metropolitan area, it is easier to talk to theater companies and get a major star to make an appearance. Sometimes, he or she is going to be in town anyway at the time of the opening. Occasionally, one of the stars visits the opening in a small town because the movie is about the area or was filmed at that location. Those are once-in-a-lifetime opportunities that make great special events.

> Giving
> opens the way
> for receiving.
>
> Florence Scovel Shinn

Live Performances

Opening nights for plays, concerts or dance performances are generally good fund-raisers because participants get the chance to see a much-anticipated performance and invest in a good cause. These events offer more opportunities to organize private receptions for "angels" or sponsors. The higher-priced tickets can include admission to a reception, and meeting key performers after the production.

Naturally, fund-raising committee members need to gauge the volunteer base and the potential ticket-buying constituency in order to assure a solid revenue potential. In addition, advertising programs, special seating and privileges for higher priced tickets, raffles and sponsorship sales all offer revenue opportunities.

Dining with a Celebrity

Many people love the opportunity to meet a celebrity, whether he or she is an expert in some area, an athlete, a well-known media notable or an individual involved in their favorite area of interest. Ideally, the celebrity has gone on to fame and fortune from the town where the agency is located. High profile, successful individuals who have ties to the community or the service agency mission are especially worth pursuing. The agency's fund-raising personnel should maintain contacts who will alert them to occasions when a sports icon or other celebrity is expected to be in town, whether to visit, work on a project or event, or promote a book, movie or television series. A dining event offers the agency a fairly simple opportunity to connect with a celebrity tour. While not every event will raise money, it will create a memorable experience and help raise awareness of the service agency's work.

In a limited number of instances, a celebrity may really care about the cause that the organization represents, and then it is possible to have a planned special event, which can include ticket sales and a gala. Tapping into the schedule of a celebrity who is an advocate for the identified cause is a matter of being in the right place at the right time. For example, Princess Yasmin, daughter of the late actress Rita Hayworth and Prince Ali Khan, is the honorary chairperson for the Alzheimer's Association's annual Rita Hayworth Gala. She brings special éclat to the events she attends and elicits large amounts of money.

One of the most disappointing aspects of planning this kind of event is that other professional obligations sometimes interfere with the celebrity's ability to make the appearance. For example, if the celebrity promises in March to appear at a benefit in late June and then signs a contract to do a long run in a play or concert, the charity may receive a call that the celebrity cannot appear. The planners and ticket purchasers are usually extremely disappointed. But, when the scheduling works, these events are great fund-raisers.

An Auction with a Luncheon or Dinner

Luncheons or dinners are popular fund-raisers, and auctions are often part of the event. The meal/auction combination can be stand-alone or coupled with another activity such as a golf tournament, dance or evening of entertainment.

Silent Auction

The silent auction can be accomplished with both donated and purchased items. Donated items are usually a safer feature because it is possible to lose money on purchased items. The big ticket items that seem to attract significant competitive bidding include trips to interesting places with airfare and lodging packages, and celebrity sports paraphernalia.

A volunteer committee should solicit the auction items from businesses and individuals. If many small items are donated, they can be attractively wrapped in clear cellophane or charming baskets and sold as a package. This is easier than trying to sell hundreds of small items. The options are innumerable–gift certificates, pieces of art, television sets, barbecues, sports equipment and tickets to events. Other good options are the use of a box at a concert or sporting event, the use of someone's vacation condo at a beach or ski resort, a ride on the donor's boat, or dinner prepared in the buyer's home by a volunteer chef and clean-up committee. The auction committee must know its audience and go for items that will sell to that market. When the auctions are held year after year, volunteers usually understand which items sell well and which ones do not attract any bids.

Setting up display tables with clearly defined, minimum opening bids and minimum raises is an important part of the planning process. A bid sheet that includes a description of the piece, the minimum opening bid, and the minimum raise should be placed on clipboards in front of each item. It should also include space for the bidder's name, the amount of the bid, the table number and a telephone number. The chairperson or emcee instructs people to bid during specific hours and then announces when the bidding is going to close, giving participants fifteen-, ten-, and five-minute warnings.

Winning bidders are notified in a variety of ways. In well-organized auctions, "runners" find winning bidders and inform them of what they have won. The bidder then goes to a cashier to pay for and pick up his items. If they are cumbersome, the bidder usually arranges for pickup or delivery in the future. Organizers sometimes have a large chalkboard or computer screen that displays the item, its number, the name of the winning bidder and the price so participants can see who won.

With a large number of biddable items, it is essential to have enough cashiers to eliminate a long wait to pay for merchandise. Making arrangements to notify those who leave the function early is another important issue. Volunteers should call within one or two days and help winners arrange for payment and item pickup.

Auctions can also be organized around themes. For example, a benefit for a local library featured a traveler's silent auction. Knowing that people who travel often buy a number of things they do not actually use when they return home, the fund-raising committee members gave participants a chance to get rid of some of their excess souvenirs. The result was baskets of beautifully wrapped items, grouped according to a particular theme and accompanied by a typed list of the basket contents. One lady put together a book basket with a few books, a pair of beautiful onyx book ends and a pretty throw from Mexico. Another basket was labeled "For baby girl age 6 to 18 months." It contained Osh Kosh B'Gosh clothes, bought during a trip to Wisconsin. The theme for another was "Tea for Two." This basket contained items bought in Ireland: two teacups, several varieties of tea and biscuits, and a book about Ireland. The baskets were put on display in the library for several weeks so that people could choose their favorite.

Live Auction

It is not unusual to feature both a silent auction and a live auction at the same event. An experienced auctioneer generally auctions off the big ticket items, while spotters placed in strategic places around the room look for raised hands. If the benefit uses preferred seating for higher priced tickets, organizers should make sure those tables are spotted carefully, since the people who buy the most expensive tickets are the most likely to bid on higher priced items.

Including a variety of entertaining, fund-raising activities in one special event can ensure that everyone has something in which to participate. When done correctly, activities can be synergistic and enhance the financial returns for the service agency.

In-Home Parties

For at least 35 years, in-home parties all held on the same night or on two or three consecutive weekends have been a common form of fund raising. It is a very effective way to make friends for the organization, if there is a core of volunteers who enjoy entertaining and do so with élan. These parties are particularly good fodder for the food page section of newspapers and local magazines, providing more publicity for the service agency.

Planning the parties is relatively simple. The fund-raising committee establishes a theme, and individual hosts and hostesses offer their homes and the food and beverages for the meal or cocktail party. Invitations are mailed out with a description of each party, including the address, the price and the number of people who can be accommodated. It is appropriate for the price of the events to vary since some will be more elaborate than others. This offers a variety of people in different circumstances the opportunity to attend. Interested persons can RSVP with a check and a reservation card that identifies which party they want to attend. Many times the host and hostess will invite their own friends to participate, and collect even more money to aid the agency. Since it is a first-come, first-served system, some parties may be overbooked.

One of the advantages to these parties is that the cost of producing them is low since the host and hostesses absorb the cost of the food, beverages and decorations. Organization expenses include the invitation printing, mailing and general publicity.

Many years ago, I gave a party in my home for a fund-raiser. Since the assigned theme was international cuisine, I chose to do a fiesta because I loved Mexico. The food, music and décor were Mexican. I bought the fresh tortillas at a tortilla factory and made tacos for eighty people, along with guacamole, flan, and other Mexican dishes. We hired a mariachi band and dancers, and rolled up the rug so people could dance. While we had to have the floor refinished after the dancers' metal-heeled shoes dug into the floor, it was a wonderful, memorable party. The *Chicago Tribune* even did a full-page article on the event and our cause.

Garden Walks

Beautiful gardens abound in many areas, and the owners are often proud to show them off. The organization's constituency may include some avid gardeners who are willing to share the beauty of their yards and flowerbeds with others to support the organization.

A selection committee should choose a number of gardens from a pool of candidates who would permit public viewing of their property. One garden walk committee asked a prominent landscaper to ask his patrons to show their gardens. The ones who agreed were flattered to have their gardens featured.

In addition to the usual ticket for entry, the planning committee should provide a map to the gardens with clearly marked addresses. Driving or walking directions should also be included, with proximity given special consideration if it is a walking tour. Some participants may make plans in advance to complete only those parts of the tour they feel comfortable walking. On the other hand, if most people drive to each location and park, special consideration should be given to traffic and parking issues.

> Be thankful
> for what you have;
> you'll end up
> having more.
>
> Oprah Winfrey

The DuPage National Association for the Mentally Ill (NAMI) created a truly successful benefit by making another option available. They hired charming red, open air trolleys and charged each person five dollars to ride from garden to garden. The trolleys left at 15-minute intervals, starting at the main check-in area and stopping at each house to let people off. After stopping at all eight gardens, the trolleys returned to the check-in location, so individuals could stay as long as they wanted. The program that was given to all participants with their map and ticket provided a brief description of each garden. In addition, two docents answered questions about the planting groups and identified plants for those interested.

The trolleys also offered the agency an added feature–a captive audience. As people boarded the trolley, a recording detailed a brief history of the organization and the programs that would benefit from the event proceeds. The following year, live commentators on each trolley described the programs and answered questions. Participants not only understood how their money would be used but also learned more about the agency itself.

NAMI used several approaches to bringing in revenue. Their ticket committee advertised the event on posters in a number of retail establishments. Committee members and several of the businesses sold tickets and collected cash. The printed program contained advertisements from many businesses. Also, advertising banners were sold for 500 dollars each and placed on either side of the six trolleys, netting another 5,000 dollars. (The printing cost for the banners was approximately 1,000 dollars.)

> Anticipate charity
> by preventing
> proverty.
>
> Maimonides

Still another small profit center was the lunch stand at the tour starting point. Volunteers sold box lunches for seven dollars each. Profits from lunches, advertising and ticket sales totaled over 25,000 dollars.

One key to success is getting the fund-raising event listed in the local newspaper's events section, and posted on a variety of public information Web sites. People need to know when and where the event will occur, and what the organization is doing. In the case of the NAMI garden walk, a publicity chairman arranged for a variety of newspaper articles and even television previews of the gardens with an interview about the cause. Many individuals who had never heard of the organization attended because they were looking for something special to do on the weekend. The affordable ticket price was another enticement. As a result of the additional publicity, others who had never heard of the cause mailed in contributions.

One major difficulty with a garden walk is, of course, the weather. Planners of the event often choose a rain date though it is an added complication. Others organize back-up plans so the event can go on even if it rains. Another difficult issue is planning the food. One option is to create two different types of tickets, one including food and one for the garden walk only. In all food planning efforts, it is important to order just enough for the correct number of ticket holders because wasted food is an expense that can be avoided.

House Walks

Organizing a house walk presents the same issues as a garden walk. Publicity, ticket distribution, food, maps and clear directions are important, as well as houses that are accessible enough to prevent large time lags between locations. Committee members may find that professionals such as interior designers and architects are most helpful in identifying homes for the tour. Another consideration is that fashion shows, garden walks and house walks are attended mostly by women. If event promoters want to attract a larger male audience, then the event should feature the homes of sports celebrities.

Privacy is an issue that individuals who consider opening their homes may wish to explore. Inviting the public to view one's home is a good deal more sensitive than having them view the garden. Some people are concerned that it offers an invitation to potential burglars, giving them the opportunity to see where valuables and access options are located. Fortunately, most people are just curious about how others live and enjoy looking at different design and decorating solutions.

Garden walks and house walks are particularly appropriate when the funds are going to provide housing for people with special needs. This link is positive and enjoyable.

Raffles

Usually used as an adjunct to an already planned special event, raffles appeal to the "let's take a chance" side of each of us. As a stand alone, fund-raising activity, it creates a special problem since raffle tickets cannot be mailed because it is a felony to use the United States mail for gaming. Some states and municipalities may even require event promoters to purchase a special license to sell tickets at the raffle. These licenses usually involve a simple application procedure and a small fee. Therefore, tickets must be sold through personal volunteer solicitation and/or sales at a special event.

The raffle chairperson and committee solicit prizes from interested community residents and businesses. Sometimes, the main prize is cash, which comes out of the event proceeds. Opinions differ on whether items or cash are better options. The argument for cash prizes is that everyone can use money, and therefore more people will buy tickets for a 500 or 1,000 dollar cash prize. In addition, the value of any prize over the amount paid is technically taxable income, so why not give the winners cash. On the other hand, some people argue that prize items enhance the value of raffle tickets. They reason that a person might think, "I would love to go on a trip like that, or buy a fur coat, diamond tennis bracelet or new set of golf clubs, but I don't want to spend that much money. So, I'll just take a chance and buy 20 dollars worth of raffle tickets. After all, it's for a good cause."

The recruitment of volunteers to sell raffle tickets is the second most important element after the selection of prizes. Organizers should choose volunteers who enjoy going up to people and asking them to buy tickets. Raffle ticket sellers should wear distinctive gear. For example, pretty girls wearing dresses with colorful sashes are nice, but if the party has a theme, their clothing should mirror it in some way. A King Midas Ball, for instance, could feature sellers wearing gold crowns, or the Mariners Gala might highlight sellers wearing captain's hats or some other item associated with seamen.

Auto Raffle

An auto raffle can be used as a stand alone, fund-raising event or a special feature at another event. These raffles are popular because many people are in the market for a new car or a specific classic model. The raffle committee should determine whether the market is greatest for a new car, a bargain, or a specific classic car model.

A limited number of tickets are usually sold at a high face value–for example, only 300 tickets at 300 dollars each for a new Cadillac. The winner may have purchased 20 tickets for a total of 6,000 dollars. If ticket sales amounted to 90,000 dollars, and the agency bought the car for 30,000 dollars from a friendly Cadillac dealer, they will net 60,000 dollars.

Raffle committee members must also keep the service agency's interests in mind. If the car is donated, the committee should determine whether it would be better to sell it to the highest bidder at a live auction or raffle it off. If the car is purchased, it is absolutely necessary to evaluate realistically how many tickets can be sold. This is possible if volunteers each commit to selling a specific number of tickets at a given price. Realistic goals prevent the worst case scenario–ticket sales that will not even cover the cost of the car purchase.

The raffle ticket should include a list of rules or information the purchaser needs to know. For example, the winner of the car must pay tax on the difference between the price of the raffle ticket(s) and the value of the car acquired. Also, purchasers are not entitled to a tax deduction. Despite some limitations, auto raffles can be effective fund-raisers for the organization.

Races and Walk-a-Thons

If the service agency has a sports-oriented cadre of volunteers, races offer a great opportunity to harness their enthusiasm. They also raise agency visibility with a new audience, promote new friendships and raise money. Races and marathons are a particularly good way to involve young people and children. Kids enjoy being sponsored for the designated cents or dollars per mile they run or laps they swim. They ask neighbors and families to sponsor them, give out pledge cards and then collect the proceeds when they have completed the event.

Another approach to use with adults is to charge an entry fee, which covers all event expenses and includes enough money to benefit the organization. Walk-a-thons and races can attract thousands of people who enjoy both the activity itself and the opportunity to compete.

For volunteers who have never planned such an event, a number of professional organizations are available to put it together for the agency. For example, the larger and more complex the event, the greater the likelihood that the fund-raising committee needs professional advice. Radio stations often sponsor charitable races, bringing entertainment and a great deal of publicity, if not revenue.

With the growing popularity of ten-kilometer "fun runs" and five-kilometer walks, some race organizers have come up with unique attractions for both runners and spectators. For example, the Park Forest (Illinois) Scenic 10K features musicians, such as a classical quartet and a bagpipe troupe, stationed at intervals along the route. Runners are treated to lovely sights and sounds as they wind their way through neighborhoods and forests.

In another example, RunOhio, an organization that serves runners in several states, organizes the Power Three 10K Series, which offers runners the chance to compete in three regional races. Any runner who enters all three is entered into a drawing to win cash prizes from 50 to 1,000 dollars. The events are sponsored by a number of businesses. One of the races, the RiteAid Cleveland Marathon and 10K, raises funds for the Boys and Girls Clubs of Cleveland and two nonprofit organizations that benefit celiac research.

Golf Tournament

The basic elements for planning a golf tournament are ticket sales to participants, sponsorships of individual holes and possibly a major sponsorship by a business that wants to cultivate the people who come to the service agency tournament. Business people will often take time away from their jobs to play in a tournament, sometimes sponsoring a foursome so they can invite customers or clients as their guests. By and large, golf tournaments appeal to male audiences far more than a house walk or garden walk.

Varying the golf course from year to year enables golfers to try different challenges and satisfy their curiosity about private club courses they may never have played on. The combination of camaraderie, the beauty of the course and the fresh air can create a very positive experience in spite of weather conditions.

The most successful tournaments not only feature prizes but also a luncheon or dinner with a silent auction and raffle. And, tournaments will often give participants the option of only joining the event for the cocktail hour and the meal. The ticket price for this option would be significantly lower since there is no need to pay green fees or rent a cart.

Typical ticket prices are 150 to 400 dollars for the golf/dinner combination and 50 to 100 dollars for just the dinner. If the service agency is able to host a large golf tournament or open event with a pro am tournament featuring celebrity players, there is a good chance that the agency can attract significant sponsorship money.

The Synergy of Special Events

Whether the service agency is located in a small community or a major metropolitan area, the combination of activities in a special event, its theme, and the enthusiasm of the volunteers are what create a positive experience for all the participants. It is also that pleasant experience plus the opportunity to give to a good cause that makes these fund-raisers such effective revenue generators. A couple of examples illustrate the success possible for enterprising service agency volunteers.

> What do we live for,
> if it is not
> to make life
> less difficult
> for each other.
>
> George Eliot

Carol Pircon, a young mother in Macomb, Illinois, chaired a 15-member committee that organized a very successful small town benefit. They decided to name the event the Flamingo Fling because the band they chose was the Flamingos. Building on the flamingo theme, they created a special drink, the Pink Flamingo; put pink flamingo decorations on each table; and required the bartenders to wear silly, pink flamingo hats with the legs hanging down on each side of their faces. (Most of the bartenders begged to keep the hats.)

They sold tickets to the Flamingo Fling and included dinner and dancing for a very modest price to ensure a large turnout. They also included a silent auction and pink flamingo raffle, with person-to-person ticket sales before and during the benefit. (Raffle tickets were all sold by men wearing black shirts with pink flamingos.) Participants played 20 minutes of bingo after dinner. A captain was appointed at each table to collect five dollars per game per person, allowing each participant ten chances to win. Dancing, the closing of the silent auction and the announcement of the raffle prize winner followed. In previous years, this benefit committee had auctioned off a trip to Disneyland, including airfare, hotel and a travel gift certificate, but they got the best raffle ticket sales from a 1,000 dollar cash prize. The breakdown of profits from the special event are listed in Table 5.1:

Table 5.1

Sale of centerpieces to a promotional firm	$1,000
Sponsorships	6,000
Underwriting of specific expenses	4,000
Raffle	5,000
Silent auction	12,000
Net ticket sales after cost of music and dinner	2,000
Net Profit	$30,000

Another successful event was the Alzheimer's ball in Chicago. Princess Yasmine Aga Kahn, daughter of Rita Hayworth and Prince Ali Khan, attended the ball along with David Hyde Pierce, who acted as the celebrity emcee. (Yasmine is supportive of Alzheimer's Association events because Hayworth suffered from the disease and died from its effects at age 68.)

Service
serves us
as well as others.

Rachel Naomi Remen

The theme of the event, held in the Chicago Lyric Opera House, was "Carmen," named after one of Rita Hayworth's films. The stage of the theater was built out for the evening to accommodate seating for 800 people. The tables were swathed in floor length, red satin tablecloths and decorated with eight-foot centerpieces of red roses. Musicians played all evening, while guests nibbled on magnificent hors d'oeuvres and placed bids on upscale auction items. The house lights dimmed to lure people from the lobby of the opera house into the main theatre where they were entertained by a 35-minute program (emceed by the wry, humorous David Hyde Pierce) and served a gourmet dinner. Needless to say, tickets to the event sold for 400 dollars.

After dinner, a live auction was held for a number of unique experiences, including golf with Princess Yasmine at Medinah Country Club in suburban Chicago. (She is a 12 handicap, so a number of bidders were intrigued with the possibility of playing with a princess who golfs so well.) That auction item sold for 4,000 dollars.

The breakdown of net revenues from the event, according to the Alzheimer's Association, is listed in Table 5.2:

Table 5.2

Ticket and table sales	$716,400
Donations	$147,489
Live auction/raffle	86,000
Silent auction	26,525
Ad journal	30,750
Gross revenue	$1,007,164
Attendance	765

(All expenses were underwritten by sponsors.)
Source: Alzheimer's Association

Obviously, events can be sponsored for any cause, and it is the combination of activities and the memory of a pleasant experience that yields the profit.

Sponsorships

Sponsorships are a source of revenue, but they are not technically a contribution. They are usually characterized as a marketing expense because something of value is given for a specific price. For example, a sponsor who is willing to give 25,000 dollars to be the exclusive "name" for a special event may want the company name printed on every invitation and ticket. The sponsor may also require that a large banner or banners (supplied by the company) with the company name on it be stretched across the entrance. The sponsoring business may also ask for ten to one hundred tickets to the best seats to provide an entertainment opportunity for its best customers. It may even want to supply a spokesperson to welcome everyone to the special event. These sponsorships are opportunities for the business to remind people in attendance of the company, its desire to serve them, and its support of the charitable organization's work to benefit the community.

When creating sponsorship opportunities, the agency attaches a price tag based on the benefits that come with the sponsorship. It must also identify the market for ticket sales. Once these steps are completed, the event committee can compile a list of potential sponsors who want to expose their products to the target audience.

The following table illustrates a typical schedule of benefits for sponsors.

Golf Tournament Schedule of Benefits

Anticipated attendance: 400 executives
Location: elite country club
Ticket price: $250 per person; $1,000 per foursome

Tournament Sponsor Benefits

- Sponsor's name included in the tournament title
- Twelve tickets for golf to be used for entertainment of customers and executives
- Banner with company name on it; full page ad inside front cover of program; name and logo on all tickets
- Permission to provide promotional merchandise to participants
- Attendance at private reception for celebrity players
- Prominent mention in all press releases
- Presentation rights for trophy winners, and photographs sent to the media
- 8 x 10 copies of photos to be sent to sponsor

Sponsorship fee $25,000

Luncheon or Dinner Sponsor Benefits

- Name of food and entertainment sponsor on large display cards on each table
- Eight tickets to golf tournament
- Twelve additional tickets for cocktail reception and meal
- Full page ad in the program
- Position in a reception line to welcome golfers and diners
- Company introduction during the proceedings and opportunity to present a trophy
- Photographs to be sent to media and sponsor
- Prominent mention in all press releases

Sponsorship fee $10,000

19th Hole Sponsor Benefits

- Name of sponsor on display card at entry to cocktail area
- Four tickets for golf tournament
- Table of ten for dinner and places for six additional guests
- Half-page ad in the program
- Position in reception line to welcome guests
- Recognition during formal proceedings and personal introduction
- Representative invited to participate in trophy presentations
- Photographs to be sent to media and sponsor
- Prominent mention in all press releases

Sponsorship fee $5,000

Individual Hole Sponsor Benefits
(18 sponsorships available)

- One ticket to play in the tournament
- Name printed on a sign at the hole
- Name and hole number listed in program on hole sponsors page
- Seat at a special table for hole sponsors

Sponsorship fee $1,000

Depending on the audience, event planners can adjust the privileges and prices of each sponsorship, though sponsorships should not be undervalued. Co-sponsorships by non-competing entities are also possible. For example, American Airlines would never co-sponsor anything with United Airlines, but it may consider doing so with an auto dealer. Organizers should remember that large corporations often have allegiances to other entities that are contractual, and they will probably not be as flexible as smaller, but still significant, local organizations.

Memorials and Honorariums

Establishing a memorial program is a simple and wonderful lead-in to a planned giving program. When someone dies who has been associated with the organization, it is fairly common to ask that contributions be made to his or her favorite charity as a memorial rather than sending flowers. The tribute lasts longer than flowers and has an immediate effect by assisting the charitable organization.

> A single act
> of kindness
> throws out roots
> in all directions, and
> the roots spring up
> and make new trees.
>
> Lawrence G. Lovasik

As with any revenue opportunities for the nonprofit, the memorial opportunity should be publicized. The easiest means is an ad or brief mention in every issue of the service agency's newsletter. The agency should also publish the names of every person who is memorialized by a contribution, along with the donor's name, in the newsletter.

When a contribution comes in, agency staff should send the donor an immediate acknowledgment of the gift. In addition, staff may choose to send individual acknowledgements to the family or a complete listing of every memorial gift received. The list should, of course, include the names of the donors. Prompt and thoughtful recognition of memorial gifts often generates still another gift from the estate or the family. If combined, the gifts may fund an annual scholarship, buy a piece of needed equipment or provide new capital improvement for the service agency.

Other memorable events such as a marriage, fiftieth wedding anniversary or graduation can be commemorated appropriately with contributions as well. The organization simply needs to let people know commemorative gifts are an option and make sure that procedures to collect and acknowledge contributions are in place.

Memberships

Some 501(c)3 organizations are membership organizations. The organization members are essentially like stockholders in a for-profit company. Members elect the board of directors at an annual meeting and have complaining rights just as stockholders do. While there may be different classes of members, membership usually entails paying an annual fee that gives each person the right to one vote. Membership fees for participation in voting tend to be modest and do not constitute a significant source of income but rather cover the cost of the annual meeting and production of an annual report, among other things. The board of directors hires the executive director who is responsible for hiring the rest of the staff. The board makes policy decisions on fiduciary issues, staff, budget recommendations and the fiscal aspects of carrying out the organization's mission.

Many of the associations for people with mental retardation, mental illness and other disabilities, such as the National Easter Seal Society, began as membership organizations and continue to operate as such. Their purpose reflected the needs of the constituency they served, with parents and relatives acting as advocates for family members.

Donor Clubs

The difference between a membership with voting rights and a donor club membership is very simple. In one, members have the right to vote; in the other, members are the means used to encourage current donors to give more generously. The more the donor club increases contributions during a given year, the higher the level of visibility and privileges they receive within the organization. The agency's fund development personnel decide how to structure and name the levels and accompanying donation amounts. Following is an example of how it works.

Table 5.3

Donor Club Schedule of Benefits

Gift Amount	Club Name	Benefits
$500	Friends	Monthly newsletter Annual report with name listed Invitations to all benefits Invitations to lunch with executive director and president of board
$1,000	Patrons	All of the above plus: VIP identification card Ten percent discount at gift shop Priority seating at all events
$2,500	Ambassadors	All of the above plus: Monthly letter from the president Special recognition at annual meeting Private luncheon with executive director and/or the board chairperson
$5,000	Life Members	All of the above plus: Seating at executive or board chairperson table for special events Private reception with supporting celebrities Name listed on donor wall at main entrance

The service agency's culture usually determines the combination of perks and recognition for the donor club members. For example, some people are averse to recognition but really enjoy the extra perks. Others enjoy the recognition and realize that they are models for emulation. In any case, the recognition and greater levels of interaction within the organization do stimulate higher levels of giving because donors feel a greater connection to the staff, the board and the work of the service agency.

6

MAINTAINING AN ACCURATE DATABASE

A major key to long-term success in donor development and recognition is using the right tools to track contributions. Every contribution from every donor should be recorded, and the staff should be able to easily create reports for board members and volunteers. The most essential management tool is computer software that tracks contributors and their contributions to each particular project. It streamlines work for the service agency fund-raising department and provides valuable analysis, summary and report capability. It is also an essential management tool.

Many database software programs are designed specifically for fund raising. The appropriate software helps fund-raising staff to communicate more effectively with customized letters, emails and thank you notes. It also produces reports, and allows the user to easily import and export large amounts of data.

> Serving, like healing,
> is mutual.
> There is no debt.
>
> Rachel Naomi Remen

Some service agencies have developed their own database software, using ACT! or Microsoft Access. While it is convenient to have customized software to meet specific needs, new challenges arise since technology keeps changing, often requiring updates and/or reprogramming. These modifications require either a costly consultant or an in-house programmer, who at some point may decide to leave. In that event, staff is left with database software that no one is trained well enough to manage. For smaller agencies, then, it is much more cost effective to acquire a multi-dimensional software program from a reputable publisher that is easy to use.

More effective database management will yield higher returns and eventually pay for the software, installation and training.

Evaluating Database Software

The Chronicle of Philanthropy is a very good source of information about fundraising software options. For example, the March 20, 2003 edition lists 15 different software products for database management. Among the most well known and widely used are Raisers Edge, GiftMaker Pro, and Exceed by Telosa. Each has advantages. Exceed has a basic compact version that interfaces with QuickBooks. It is quite reasonably priced, which works for the small nonprofit. GiftMaker Pro manages constituents, processes gifts, provides for organizational mailing needs, and creates reports that analyze fund-raising efforts. It also offers a program that allows the organization to receive online donations securely. Raisers Edge publishers promote it as a complete fund-raising system that allows users to do contact management, communicate with constituents, and track the success and cost of each campaign. It also integrates with Microsoft Outlook's calendar and performs mail merges in Microsoft Word.[1]

Given the choices and agency needs, choosing the right package is a major issue. Following are some of the factors that agency staff should consider as they review the choices available.

- Is it easy to operate?
- Does it have the capability to address the issues of greatest concern to the agency?
- Can it store photographs of donors?
- Is good technical support and training available?
- How does it integrate with the operating system already in place at the agency?
- Is it possible to import data from other programs, such as client names and addresses?
- How much does it cost?

- Will it save money in administration after the initial installation and training by producing the kinds of reports the agency needs?
- Does the company selling the software have a track record and is it financially stable? (Once installed, software glitches may create enormous problems should the company go out of business.)

The best place to look at software is at national or regional conferences, since the software publishers usually demonstrate their products for attendees. They generally give visitors a brief demonstration and allow them to use the software for a short time. After sampling several products, agency staff can make comparisons and get a better idea of the kind of software that would fit the organization's needs. After conferring with those who will be using the software, agency management can make an informed decision.

Training on Database Software

The latest generation of fund-raising software has amazing capabilities. Staff members have so much to absorb during the initial training sessions that most users are on overload and need to take time to reinforce what they have learned by using the software for a while. Further training, whether on-site or off-site, should be made available to the fund development staff and the chief information officer. Training and online or telephone support are often included in the software purchase. The agency should definitely buy the entire package, so staff members can continue to expand their skills.

Protecting the database from corruption–the entry of misinformation or changing of correct data by unauthorized persons–is a real problem for anyone working with databases. The accuracy of data entry is of utmost importance; therefore, agency management should take the proper precautions to ensure that only competent, reliable people have access to the database. While part-time employees and interns are sometimes assigned the data entry job, it is safer to have only one or two trained employees managing the database.

Essential Database Information

The most important fields of information include:

Donor listings
- Prospect's name
- Volunteer solicitor or main contact person
- Dates when they were contacted and when they contributed
- Address(es) (home, business, summer and winter locations, and post office box)
- Telephone
- Fax
- Email
- Notes
- Cross references (for example, *Donor is principal of ABC Foundation, executive director of DEF Corporation, actively involved in the Rotary Club.*)

Categories for individual appeals
- Annual appeal
- Golf tournament
- Gala tickets
- Fashion show
- Sponsorship of gifts

Constituency code
- Individual
- Business
- Foundation
- Staff
- Alumni/client
- Family member

Other categories could include grants, mailings and/or events.

The software should enable the staff to generate reports correspnding to a number of criteria–by date, for example. Or, the report might list all donations for the year, alphabetically by individual name or by business name. Or, the board of directors might request a report of all donors for the past five years by donation amount, cumulatively. See Table 6.1.

Table 6.1

Donor Groupings

A typical grouping of donors
by dollar amount donated over a five-year period

$ 100 –	$ 499
500 –	999
1,000 –	4,999
5,000 –	9,999
10,000 –	24,999
25,000 –	49,999
50,000 and higher	

Reports are enormously helpful when compiling all names and gifts by individual fund-raising effort (for example, all contributors to last year's golf tournament). They form the basis for possibly upgrading the level of participation for the current year.

Individual profiles of donors are also important because development staff may need to know what interests a specific donor has. For instance, a donor may have given 10,000 dollars over the past three years in connection with special events. Another may have given 10,000 dollars over the same period of time in response to an annual appeal. Conversations are usually more productive when the staff is structuring a campaign and has the giving history of the donor. For example, the agency fund-raiser can say, "We are very grateful for your support of the annual appeal, and without affecting that gift, we were wondering if it might be possible to have your company sponsor some phase of the agency golf tournament. The sponsorship would provide name recognition for you and entertainment opportunities for the business." Or, he might say, "We greatly appreciate your 500 dollar contribution during the annual appeal, but we are having a special drive for a new physical therapy room. We're wondering if you would consider increasing that to 1,000 dollars."

Confidentiality

Determining who will have access to the donor files is a sensitive issue. The database is a major asset of the organization and should be treated as such. It is equivalent to a for-profit organization customer and prospect list. In most cases, only those people who are directly working on fund raising–the staff in the development department, the executive director and the chief financial officer–should manage the files.

In many large organizations, volunteers who are doing the "ask" for a specific event or campaign are equipped with a full donor history of contributions for the individuals they are calling. Naturally, anonymous donors are treated differently. Their records require special attention so the coding enables their gifts to be listed in reports as anonymous.

In addition, the chair of an annual appeal or a benefit will probably want to see who gave the year before and how much the donation was. The information helps him decide whether a donor should be asked to join the fund-raising committee, and how to approach the person during the current campaign. Also, in the process of reviewing donor files, the chair will likely recognize a number of names and make comments like, "George only gave 500 dollars. He can do better than that. I'll ask Al to talk to him."

Ideally, the database user should have access only to files necessary to the work he is doing at the time. The development director may decide, for example, that computer savvy users may have passwords and access to the files in read-only capability. This ensures that only the person(s) most highly skilled at data entry and data management will be able to make changes. While this works most of the time, occasionally a user may need to add dates, or notes about contacts and results.

Keeping Current

The tedious but essential process of eliminating duplications and keeping addresses up to date on the agency mailing list must be done at the very least once a year. Nothing angers donors or volunteers more than receiving two or three copies of the newsletter or any individual mailing because they appear on more than one of the agency's lists. They see each duplication as a complete waste of time and the money they helped to raise.

One technique for updating databases is to print out hard copies of different categories of people–clients, alumni, family, staff, donors and volunteers, for instance–and ask staff to check for overlap between the listings. The people who work most closely with each category should compare the lists to their own records and make corrections in pen or pencil. This can be difficult because some donors request that a mailing be sent to both their business and their home. The greatest responsibility falls on the director of development, who knows that E. T. Smith, a volunteer, and Elizabeth Smith are the same person. Furthermore, Elizabeth is also Mrs. Bertran Smith, a family member and donor, who receives mail in another category under Mr. and Mrs. Bertran Smith. Only someone who has a full overview of the donor base would know that information. That is why even the best computer program is an efficient and powerful tool only when it is in the right hands.

> Charity
> begins at home
> and justice
> begins next door.
>
> Charles Dickens

Once the lists have been corrected, the master list should be delivered to the main data entry person within a specified period of time. Since the data entry process is so tedious, it may be necessary to include a reminder from the executive director that emphasizes the importance of keeping the information up to date. If the staff person sees it as less urgent, he may put the list at the bottom of the work pile because daily operations appear to be more pressing.

When selling or liquidating, a for-profit business lists its assets as the buildings, equipment, inventory, key staff and the customer list. Sometimes, the purchasing entity buys the other assets, but it almost always requests the customer list. The service agency donor database is equivalent to that customer list. It is valuable not only because the list provides the agency with fund-raising contacts, but also because other nonprofits are willing to pay to use it on an annual basis for their own mailings. Those outside offers are hard evidence of the database's significance even though it has no value on the agency balance sheet. Agency management should treat the donor database as the major asset that it is and allocate the resources necessary to keep it both accurate and current.

The CAN-SPAM Act

With current technology, many service agencies can now maintain contact with their constituents via email. Agencies must comply with the requirements of the CAN-SPAM Act, which became law in December of 2003. The law enables the consumer to choose to prevent further unsolicited emails (or spam) from a sender.[2] It states specifically that it is illegal to send an unsolicited commercial email unless the message includes the following: "(1) a 'clear and conspicuous identification that the message is an advertisement or solicitation' (not necessarily in the email subject line); (2) an ability to opt-out electronically from future emails; and (3) a valid postal address of the sender."[3] In spite of the ruling, nonprofits should experience little impact since emails with a "transactional or relationship content" are exempt. The ruling also exempts emails with commercial content as long as they include a "transactional or relationship" message at the beginning of the email and do not refer to advertisements or promotions in the subject line.[4]

> Happiness, freedom, and peace of mind are always attained by giving them to someone else.
>
> Peyton Conway March

The following regulations clarify the nonprofit's responsibilities.

- The law defines commercial email as messages with the primary purpose of selling products. Email newsletters are not classified as commercial email, even when they have ads.

- The law refers to "senders" of commercial, electronic messages, such as an advertiser who is promoting his products or services. The identity of the email's sender must be clear because the sender is responsible for deleting the address of anyone who unsubscribes from the database. Companies with several divisions, each with its own publishing division, must ensure that all divisions honor any request to unsubscribe. This may not, however, apply to a sister company or corporations.

- While the new law does not require an email sender to get the recipient's permission before sending a message, obtaining permission first is still the best practice.

- Ads must still adhere to specific Federal Trade Commission (FTC) guidelines. The FTC disclosure guidelines for Internet ads can be found at www.ftc.gov.

- The law states that the sender must delete an address within ten business days of receiving the unsubscribe message.

- Emails should also include a reminder to subscribers stating the reason why they are receiving the messages. The reminder should include the sender's name, postal address and working unsubscribe link.[5]

The full text of the law or a summary of the regulations can be found at www.spamlaws.com.

7

CREATING AN ALUMNI ASSOCIATION

In the United States, the word "alumni" usually refers to the male and female graduates of colleges, universities and other private schools. While not classified as educational institutions, many human service agencies produce "alumni." They serve people with significant disadvantages, such as disabling conditions, addictions, abusive homes/families, developmental disabilities, chronic mental illness and sometimes a combination of these problems. As a result, the agencies nurture human development and teach the skills that are needed to survive in a practical sense–daily living skills, communication, money-handling skills and medication compliance.

> Even if I knew that tomorrow the world would go to pieces, I would still plant my apple tree.
>
> Martin Luther

The "graduates" of these organizations experience growth that is not measured by a degree or a piece of paper. Usually, they are truly successful if they are able to become largely self-supporting. However, the likelihood that they will able to make large gifts to the organization in recognition of the role it played in shaping their lives is quite small since the conditions from which they suffer often include the additional challenges of poverty.

Even so, alumni associations for service agencies can be formed. Those who move through the portals of these organizations are indeed pupils who have been nourished and cared for by staff. Sometimes, their families are as much a part of the alumni as the individual. So, the association can serve both the former client and the entire family, depending on the mission of the agency and the target population it serves.

Needless to say, significant obstacles must be overcome. In many, though not all instances, clients receiving services move on with their lives and lose touch with their old friends. Some alumni who remain in the community choose to maintain connections with old acquaintances, while others remain connected because they need the agency's services all of their lives. Furthermore, anyone in the field of serving people with mental retardation and mental illness knows the pattern of closing institutions, uprooting and traumatizing vulnerable people, and separating them from the only persons with whom they have had relationships. While one hopes that the less restrictive environments in which they are placed will offer the opportunity for more freedom and development, the vagaries of state funding and the reclassifying of diagnoses and developmental needs often pull an individual from one program into another located elsewhere.

> It is possible
> to give without loving,
> but it is impossible
> to love
> without giving.
>
> Richard Braunstein

The lack of connection also affects those who have dealt with addictions. They know the loss of relationships because of their dependence on some unhealthy coping style. Still others have experienced homelessness and find themselves cut off from their past support system of co-workers, family and friends.

For example, one large agency in Illinois serves over 900 clients in programs that cover five different counties. A recent examination of the client list by name, place of origin and last referral revealed that only one third of them came from a community within that five-county area. The remaining 70 percent were from other parts of the state, out of state, or the city of Chicago. In a significant number of cases, there was no birth certificate in existence. The "system" had no knowledge of the birth parents, or date and location.

The need to maintain some semblance of roots is a deep longing within all people. They need to feel a sense of community in the present and work to keep those connections into the future.

The human service agency can help alumni maintain those connections. Just as it plans events to keep volunteers a cohesive group and give them recognition, the agency should provide opportunities for clients and families to feel a continued sense of belonging even after they have moved on with their lives. An annual alumni reunion can help renew old friendships and remind the people who received services what the organization continues to do for others who face similar challenges. Though service agencies would have relatively few people at a fiftieth reunion because of the high percentage of disabling conditions, a good number might attend a ten-year, twenty-year or twenty-five-year reunion. The reunion could be organized to coincide with the year of attendance, or the anniversary of the day the client entered the agency. Reunions should include parents and other family members, but in many cases the alumni are the entire family.

While the reunion serves the valuable function of keeping people connected, it also offers alumni the opportunity to inspire and help others. The agency can invite "successful" alumni to come and talk about their lives in a group situation, possibly inspiring current clients to greater achievements. Alumni could also participate in fund-raising activities. For example, they could help raise money for a classroom, garden walk, kitchen or gym. Family members might need to be involved, but the alumni will likely experience a significant sense of accomplishment regardless. In addition, they will have the chance to give and share from their own resources of time and/or money.

When there is sufficient interest in creating an alumni association, several factors must be addressed. First, the agency should establish and maintain a database of names and addresses. Each entry should identify the person as a client, parent, sibling, other family member, nurturer or professional staff member. A section for notes helps track who attended events, who likes to volunteer, when a person was last served by the agency and so on. Since the software for fund raising and other mailings has the capacity to store and categorize all sorts of information, the alumni data may be maintained by the department of development. Updating the client's personal and family information as he or she moves to greater levels of independence is critical. Address and other data changes may be communicated through the caseworker or program contact.

The agency newsletter can be a vehicle for communicating dates and locations of alumni meetings or reunions. By coding all of the alumni entries in the database, the newsletter can be sent to them without incurring too much extra expense.

Limited finances may dictate that the alumni reunion occur only once a year. The community education or fund-raising department can make arrangements for the reunion since special events are generally in their purview. Any program staff members willing to help should be involved in organizing the event. Having the staff members call the clients who have moved on to more independent living situations is especially effective because a familiar voice saying, "We'd like to see you again" is a touch of warmth that promotes the continued connection. Clients and family members can also make some of the calls.

Since the primary function of the alumni reunion is to create a sense of continuity and commitment, the cost of tickets and participation should be just enough to cover expenses. Clients with limited resources will also benefit from the lower ticket price. Some donors may wish to underwrite complimentary tickets for the alumni who cannot even afford the basic cost. These donations may also help cover the cost of staff time involved in planning the event.

Reunion organizers should remember that the purpose of the event is to promote a sense of community, allowing clients to remain connected with people who helped them along the journey toward greater development and independence.

8

ATTRACTING MAJOR DONORS

"Generosity is not a luxury in this country," says Claire Gaudiani. "It is a cultural norm, a defining characteristic of our successful economy."[1] His statement is not simply an opinion; there are statistics to support it. An analysis by Paul Schervish and John Havens at Boston College indicates that "4.97 percent of families in the United States with a net worth of one million dollars accounted for forty-two percent of donations to charitable organizations in 1997."[2] In addition, "0.4 percent of the bequests from estates of over twenty million dollars accounts for fifty-eight percent of the value of all bequests"[3]

Clearly open-handed, American donors give for a variety of reasons. Some give to help others because they feel fortunate and want to make the world a better place. Others give simply for ego satisfaction or because they want to be remembered. Still others want to follow the lead of friends and acquaintances in sharing a common

> If you have much,
> give of your wealth.
> If you have little,
> give of your heart.
>
> Arab proverb

goal and supporting a worthwhile cause. Another group of people gives because it is a reflection of personal religious beliefs, while yet other individuals give because a respected friend or associate requests a donation for a specific cause. People also give because compelling needs strike an emotional chord or the stated solution for the problem is convincing. And finally, people give for an array of complicated personal reasons. Giving is clearly a very personal manifestation of a person's core beliefs and value systems.

Major donors seem to abound, but where are they? In 2000, there were 56,582 foundations registered (that is, had filed a Form 990PF) with the IRS.[4] But, many more people who do not necessarily have foundations make major gifts.

Defining a Major Donation

The logical question to ask is: "What is a major donor?" Is it, for example, someone who has given 5,000 dollars over the last five years, or more like 10,000 or 50,000? The field narrows when one considers people who have the capacity to make million-dollar gifts. Not everyone is philanthropically inclined, so individuals who will make million-dollar gifts in their lifetime are an even smaller group.

The Chronicle of Philanthropy listed America's 40 biggest donors for 2002, who gave gifts ranging from 17 million to 1.38 billion dollars (which was a bequest).[5] The following year, those numbers rose; the top 40 donors gave between 20 million and 1.91 billion dollars. In both years, the largest gifts were the result of a series of bequests. In 2002, the bequests came from the estate of Walter Annenberg, and in 2003 from the estate of Joan Kroc.[6] Also in 2003, *Forbes* magazine listed 222 billionaires in the United States. They did not all appear in the top 40 list; only ten were named. However, many of those billionaires have their own foundations and will give generously over a lifetime. In any case, donors all need a cause and the inclination to make a major gift.[7]

> Whoever renders service to many puts himself in line for greatness.
>
> Philip Gibbs

Donors in the Agency Database

So, how does the human service agency attract major donors? Basic to the process is finding donors whose vision aligns with the agency's vision, mission and fundraising needs. The best place to begin the search is in the agency's constituency because these are people who have already shown an interest in supporting the agency's work. Using the current database, agency staff should examine the giving patterns of everyone listed. Following are some pertinent questions to ask during the search.

- Who has been giving regularly?
- Who has the capacity to make large gifts?
- Who has the inclination to make major gifts to the agency?
- If the donor has given only once years ago, who made the contact that resulted in a donation?
- To what appeal did the one-time donor respond?
- Do any members of the agency constituency remember the circumstances of the prospect's involvement?
- Does the donor software have the capacity to track any of the details of the gift(s)?

The next step is to ask agency board members, volunteers and staff to identify donors who have the ability to make larger gifts. Other sources of potential donors are community newspapers and newsletters. They run public announcements of significant donations, which can provide potential donor names. The development department should always check the database to see if any of the names that surface are already in the system.

If a donor who is already giving to the agency makes a larger gift to another community project, development staff should identify what causes she supports. The logical progression is to discover how the agency mission fits into her areas of interest by asking whether the agency currently has a program that might appeal to her. Staff should also consider what vision the agency has to expand its service capacities if the funds became available.

Table 8.1

The Super Philanthropists of 2002

*($17 million to $1.38 billion in gifts given by
fifty-four living donors and eight bequests)*

The groups receiving gifts included:

- 45 colleges and universities
- 20 hospitals and medical centers
- 16 foundations
- 13 arts groups
- 9 education groups
- 7 environmental and animal-related groups
- 7 museums and libraries
- 6 international organizations
- 3 human services groups
- 2 donor advised funds
- 2 health charities
- 2 public affairs groups
- 2 religious groups
- One community foundation
- One historic preservation group
- One Jewish federation
- One operating foundation
- One science group
- One sports and recreation organization

From *The Chronicle of Philanthropy* (February 20, 2003).[8]

The next issue to address is how to approach the potential donor. Who asks for the gift is critical. Ideally, it should be someone the prospective donor knows and respects. While it is always appropriate for the chief executive officer (CEO) or the board chair to be involved in the "ask," another individual who knows the prospect could help the agency determine who should be at the initial meeting. The person could be a staff member who has a close relationship with the prospect or a volunteer. The CEO's and the development officer's job is to develop closer ties to the donor after the initial meetings. They should consider sending not only the usual newsletter but also the president's monthly letter, directed only to selected individuals. (See "Membership.")

Arranging a tour of the agency operations is the next step. Agency personnel should execute the tour carefully, respecting the prospective donor's time. Then, the development staff involved in the negotiations should collect enough information to present a proposal that meets the donor's interests. The negotiation process may require several follow-up meetings before a gift is finally made. This is not a short process. Matching expectations and needs takes time and understanding.

Gifts provided by well-known people in the community give the agency an important advantage. They lend the organization and its cause a higher level of credibility. And, they often inspire other prominent people to give. Therefore, it is well worth the agency's time and resources to cultivate, involve and inspire them to give in a significant way.

Donors Outside the Agency Database
If an agency still needs major gifts after working with the donors within its current constituency, the development department should consider contacting other people in the area. Unfortunately, a number of factors can make the search for new donors time-consuming and difficult. A successful fund-raising campaign starts with an understanding of these factors.

A service agency that is located in a community with demographics below the poverty line will likely face a number of challenges. The people it serves have very limited resources, and their families have barely enough resources for survival and often have no contact with them. In addition, board members may also have limited resources, including no contact with people who are comfortable enough financially to make large donations. The good news is that these agencies are most apt to be located in a large metropolitan area, where corporate and philanthropic organizations can work to help them strengthen their boards and find foundation grants.

Service agencies in areas with mid-level demographics often face a different and equally difficult challenge. They may have great difficulty soliciting major gifts because foundations often focus their resources and energy on the neediest people in the inner city. Suburbs and other outlying communities are frequently ignored. Since the mission of these agencies is to serve the community in which they are located, the client base cannot be changed appreciably. But, agency administrators and staff can begin to reach out to families who have means and also offer to serve their family members. In fact, the best prospect for a major donation is the wealthy family who is served by the agency. Sometimes, a major gift does not occur until the death of the client or the senior family members, so setting up a deferred or planned giving program is very important.

Because of their small, defined areas, rural communities are able to keep closer track of residents who are capable of donating. However, they have a greater need to partner with other organizations in joint fund raising, so they can cover a broader territory and expand their ability to tap into certain funding sources. For example, two or three charities that share similar populations in adjacent geographic areas might plan their major gift program together and also share staff.

Whenever it is possible, the agency development department should search for individuals who are making large gifts to other causes. In addition to traditional sources such as personal friends of agency constituents and the media, staff should search country club lists (usually available only through a member), and the annual reports of other charitable organizations. In addition, agency board members, fund-raising committee members and staff can make suggestions for other potential donors. If board members and volunteers do not have frequent contact with wealthy potential donors, it is essential to begin recruiting individuals who do. This process is very gradual, so it is important to do it "early and often," as the saying goes.

Another step organizations have taken to develop more contacts with the moneyed set is to recruit a development staff person who is familiar with the power structure of the community and is already connected to some philanthropists. These would include someone who is a member of the family of a bank president or high ranking trust officer, the president of a major business, a family member of long-established wealth, a major land owner or a major building developer. It is ideal, of course, to recruit that person for the position of director of development, providing she has the essential knowledge and experience in fund raising. But, a position in the next tier down can be equally valuable to the organization.

Other sources of contacts for potential donors are centers of influence in the community such as bankers, trust officers, accountants, attorneys, financial planners, financial advisors, family wealth counselors, investment bankers and people involved in the political process. Privately held companies may also be sources of donations, though if they are not publicly traded, the stockholders cannot easily sell shares of stock and so may be limited to gifts through the company or its foundation.

Furthermore, lists of names are available from a variety of marketing sources. However, list users must be cautious because the data usually reflects spending patterns rather than true income and family net worth. Realistically, most people are very private about their financial matters, and it is quite common for people with incomes in the millions to write "Income: $10,000 plus per year" on any application forms, including the U.S. Census. Also, people who are struggling may write "$80,000 a year" on a credit card application. As a result, they appear on the list as individuals with money.

Service agency administrators should consider starting an advisory board to help exclusively with fund raising. It is good policy to promote these board members to the main policy board when possible. In fact, as positions open up on the board of directors, it is wise to make fund-raising capability and willingness to give a requirement. Many boards have an annual minimum gift requirement for each of their board members. Finally, development personnel can even consider making an appointment to see local philanthropists to lay the agency cause before them and ask for help. If there are no board volunteers, the point is just to start. Development staff should not waste time wringing their hands and bemoaning the lack of contacts. They must take the first step and make a contact.

Cultivating the potential donor can be done in a variety of ways. (See also activities listed in Chapter 5: Donor Clubs.) The process might begin with an invitation to tour the service agency programs and become familiar with its work. Agency personnel should also send a monthly newsletter, the annual report, invitations to all benefits with a note from a board member or the executive director, and invitations to lunch with the executive director and the chairman of the board. In addition, they could provide priority seating at any special events the potential donor chooses to attend.

> Blessed are those
> who can give
> without remembering
> and take
> without forgetting.
>
> Elizabeth Asquith
> Bibesco

The request for an initial gift might be presented as an invitation to join one of the donor club membership levels. Or, it might be an invitation to a special event. The individual making the initial contact attempts to determine which approach would interest the donor most. The key is always finding out which agency programs or initiatives are most appealing. The reality is that most people give major gifts to the organizations they care about. Agency personnel should never assume that they can just ask for a major gift without educating donors in a thoughtful way.

Donors of One Million Dollars or More

Wealthy individuals have a variety of concerns, as we all do, about their family members, their health and managing their money. In addition, philanthropic individuals sometimes consider charitable giving as important as concern for the financial well-being of their family and heirs. These individuals may give major gifts through estate planning partly for tax purposes, partly because of control issues and partly because they want to say thank you or just be remembered.

My husband and I have made a few observations of our own, noting the connection between wealth and giving. We selected 111 individuals we know personally, representing 76 families who have wealth of ten million to four billion dollars. We separated them into Philanthropic Group A, persons who have given at least one million dollars to one individual charity during their lifetime, and Philanthropic Group B, persons who have never made a gift over 500,000 dollars to one charity during their lifetime. We also indicated whether the wealth was first, second, third or fourth generation.

Table 8.2

Families with Wealth of $10 Million to $4 Billion
Philanthropic Group A
(Gifts of $1,000,000 or more)

1st Generation	2nd Generation	3rd Generation	4th Generation
31	9	4	1

Philanthropic Group B
(Gifts of less than $1,000,000)

1st Generation	2nd Generation	3rd Generation	4th Generation
24	5	2	0

Philanthropic Group A

The stories of each family represented in the groups are many, fascinating and varied. Among the people in Group A, there is one individual whose first generation wealth amounts to ten million dollars. He was an inventor and engineer and gave over two million dollars in his lifetime and had another three million desig-nated for charity at his death. He made the money himself, was raised in a family who valued sharing and carried on the tradition. His focus was a very specific area related to education.

Another person, from third generation wealth, gave five million dollars in his lifetime to causes dear to his heart. Then, he left a 25-million-dollar estate, which his children (the fourth generation) fought over. They fired the trustee and nothing went to charity. In fact, most of the money went to attorneys' fees, with a minimal distribution of funds to the fourth generation. A large distribution had been planned for a skipping trust to the fifth generation that amounted to another 25 million.

Despite these unfortunate outcomes, at this man's death, he left an incredible legacy to his local community because of his intellectual and personal involvement in conservation efforts. He also conserved a significant amount of money for his grand-children even though he could not do so for his children, who fought his wishes after his death even though he had divided assets according to their own stated desires.

One lovely lady, whose wealth was third generation, gave 30 percent of her income each year to charity. That part of her 20-million-dollar estate flowed into a foundation. Her heirs are interested in philanthropy, but not social services, which was her focus. They support their own causes.

Also included in Group A are a successful industrialist and his wife, whose pri-mary concerns were funding for their religious interests and the arts. They took four million dollars from their 15-million-dollar estate to set up a foundation. Within ten years, they had given away the entire four million and made additional provi-sions for the charities of their choice after their death. It is interesting to note that these were not the same charities they had originally named in their wills 40 years earlier. People's passions, interests and priorities change over time.

Another successful businessman included in Group A sold the controlling interest in his business for 50 million dollars and established a foundation with 18 million. Deeply concerned about the plight of immigrants, he gave away four million in the first three years to local social service agencies working with the immigrant popu-lation in his local community.

In addition, one of the few billionaires with whom we are acquainted set up a major foundation capitalized at approximately 150 million dollars to fund organizations that address environmental issues. It was one of the projects he took on in his seventies.

In our study, the beneficiaries of the majority of the gifts of one million dollars or more were individual colleges and universities. The families' interests were and are educational, religious, artistic, environmental, health-related and human service oriented.

Philanthropic Group B

These are people who are second or third generation wealth, some of whom have siblings in Group A. So far, they have not chosen to make major gifts to a single charity. They will underwrite a special event for 20,000 dollars, buy a table at a gala for 5,000 or give 20 organizations 5,000 each, but they do not make one million dollar commitments. They would still be considered major donor prospects, but at least in their lifetimes do not feel the same compulsion to share their wealth as those in Group A. Service agency personnel will not know the difference until volunteers and staff begin to get acquainted with prospective donors as individual human beings. Having the reserves to give a million dollars does not necessarily translate into being philanthropic or charitable.

Donors of 50,000 to 500,000 Dollars

According to the AAFRC Trust for Philanthropy/Giving USA 2003, 240.92 billion dollars in contributions during 2002 and 240.72 billion in 2003 were allocated as follows.

Table 8.3

Contribution Comparison for 2002-2003

2002	2003
• 35% to religion	34% to religion
• 13.1% to education	13% to education
• 7.7% to human services	8% to human services
• 7.8% to health	9% to health
• 4.8% to public-society benefit	6% to public-society benefit
• 5.1% to arts, culture and humanities	5% to arts, culture and humanities
• 2.7% to environment/animals	3% to environment/animals
• 1.9% to international affairs	2% to international affairs
• 9.1% to foundations	11% to foundations
• 12.6% to unallocated giving	19% to unallocated giving

Source: AAFRC Trust for Philanthropy, www.aafrc.org (accessed October 2004)

These donations include gifts of all sizes. In addition, *The Chronicle of Philanthropy* did a study based on IRS records of Americans earning 50,000 dollars or more who itemized their deductions. Those taxpayers donated 97 billion dollars, about 80 percent of the total 122 billion donated by all individuals in 1997. They determined that this group gave an average of 6.4 percent of its discretionary income annually, with the major portion of that going to religious giving. Interestingly, their study showed that contributions expressed as a percentage of disposable income went down as income rose. It also indicated that people in the East give significantly less (2.7 percent), than people in the Midwest (5.0 percent), the South (9 percent) and the West (5.7 percent). This reinforces the theory that everyone is different, and distinct geographical areas have different approaches.[9]

The Secret Treasure

Individuals on the agency board and in the rest of the constituency who give generously are vitally important. But, the individuals who brought them into the organization are the agency's secret treasures. Yes, people give to good causes, but more importantly, they most often give to people they know and respect. Individual contacts may not themselves be able to give in a major way, but they are sincere, effective persons who care about the agency's mission and move in circles that touch people with deep pockets. The agency as a whole should cultivate, honor and treasure them because they are key to the agency's future.

9

UNDERSTANDING FOUNDATIONS

Organizations classified as nonprofit under the IRS tax codes are vastly different. Many exist for the benefit of people with similar interests, such as clubs, trade associations, social organizations and labor unions. Section 501 of the IRS tax code explains in detail the tax exemption on other nonprofits such as corporations and trusts (Title 26, Subtitle A, Chapter 1, Subchapter F, Part 1, Section 501). They include community chests, and entities organized and operated exclusively for religious, charitable, scientific, testing for public safety, literary or educational purposes. Others in the same category are civic leagues, clubs, fraternal organizations, teachers retirement fund associations, benevolent life insurance associations, credit unions, cemetery companies, domestic building and loan associations, and mutual savings banks.

> Seek joy
> in what you give,
> not in what you get.
>
> Author unknown

The tax code differentiates between these organizations–which are exempt from certain taxes and are not subject to income taxes–and organizations that may receive contributions that are tax deductible to the donor. Organizations classified as 501(c)3 must meet the IRS's rigid public support tests, also known as IRC sections 509 9a0920 and 170 9b09109A0(vi), in order to legally offer the broadest range of deductibility to donors. The task of meeting these requirements is onerous, but the goal is basic. The nonprofit must demonstrate that a vast majority of the support comes from many contributors and other public sources, such as grants from public taxing bodies (that is, state, municipal, county or federal government). Most human service agencies that provide direct services are paid with tax dollars and therefore easily meet the test. However, private and corporate foundations receive their donations from a limited number of sources, and are subject to careful scrutiny through an array of rules and taxes. Table 9.1 illustrates the difference in deductibility limitations for private non-operating foundations and supporting organizations. There are no such limitations for 501(c)3 organizations.

Table 9.1

Private Foundation Versus Supporting Organization

	Private Foundation (Non-Operating)	Supporting Organization IRC Sec. 509(a)(3)
Deductibility limitations		
Value of appreciated assets	Cost basis at time of transfer	Market value at time of transfer
Qualified stock	Market value	Market value
Deductions allowable in tax year		
Gifts of cash	Up to 30% of AGI	Up to 50% of AGI
Gifts of appreciated assets	Up to 20% of AGI	Up to 30% of AGI
Carryover of deduction	Maximum 5 years	Maximum 5 years
Tax restrictions - excise taxes		
Tax on net investment income	Yes	No
Tax on self-dealing	Yes	No
Tax on failure to distribute income	Yes	No
Tax on excess business holdings	Yes	No
Tax on jeopardy investments	Yes	No
Tax on taxable expenditures	Yes	No

Gifts of qualified appreciated stock are fully deductible up to fair market value IRC Sec. 170(e)(5)(c). The deduction of the full market value of qualified appreciated stock by one donor is limited to ten percent of the stock of the corporation.

Source: Nelson-Walker, *Planned Giving for Social Service Agencies*.[1]

Many individuals, on first entering the field of fund raising as professionals or as volunteers, assume that the way big money is raised is to write to foundations, identify the service agency's projected need(s), and wait for a check. They might also consider inviting people from the foundation to see their good work.

The reality is that an enormous number of organizations call themselves foundations. Many of them are not foundations that give money away at all, and most of them do not give to outside 501(c)3 organizations. In fact, a large number are soliciting money for their own causes.

Foundations are extremely varied organizations. The most common ones (public charities) include the name "foundation" in their own names. These are 501(c)3 organizations that run programs and raise money from the public and other foundations. Other public entities, such as schools that have traditionally been supported completely by tax dollars, are now establishing support foundations (for example, the Roosevelt Middle School Foundation or the School District 153 Foundation). They encourage people to make charitable gifts so they can enhance programs that can no longer be maintained with tax dollars. This type of support organization can also offer the full benefits of 501(c)3 status to its donors.

A second includes private foundations (non-operating) defined in IRS Code Section 4942. These foundations are subject to a variety of restrictions and taxes. Many of them are set up by a single individual or family (the grantor), and their main activity usually consists of making grants to 501(c)3 entities. Sometimes, these are referred to as private family foundations. Often, the original grantor who provided the money to fund the foundation will choose other family members as board members. The family continues to fund the foundation with their own money and choose the charities to which they make donations. The original donor usually sets the priorities and purpose of the foundation.

Gifts to the foundation are regulated by law. Cash, of course, is always given at face value. The only appreciated asset that can be transferred to a private foundation with full market value deductibility is a gift of qualified stock. Qualified stock is classified as publicly traded stock or stock for which market quotations are readily available. There is, however, a limitation that cumulative contributions of the stock of any one company by any one individual cannot exceed ten percent of the value of all the corporation's outstanding stock. All other gifts of appreciated property to a private foundation are treated as deductible only on their basis. In other words, whatever the donor paid for that asset is the amount he or she can deduct for tax purposes.

A third type of foundation is only part of a corporation. These foundations have some unique characteristics, though they operate with the same restrictions discussed above. They often have limited assets and are funded each year from corporate profits. They may fund areas of specific interest to the top executives or provide matching gifts to causes that individual employees support. Some corporate foundations own significant amounts of the publicly traded company stock and represent a significant voice in corporate policy. Since the stock holdings are significant, the giving level is usually significant as well. The Hewlett Packard Foundation is one example of such a foundation.

> He who obtains
> has little.
> He who scatters
> has much.
>
> Lao-Tzu

Community foundations, a fourth type, receive grants or endowments from large donors. Often, they manage donor-advised funds for individuals who do not want the hassle of operating a private foundation but want to make gifts when it is most advantageous to them for tax purposes. Over a period of time, they can recommend donations to organizations or general causes they would like to support. Fortunately for donors, a significant number of community foundations will permit recommendations from their donors on specific charities and programs, and will agree to give the money. Another significant number of community foundations consider only broad guidelines in making gifts, and will not accept gifts that are limited to any specific charity or sum of money. The rationale for this approach is varied but often the foundation board believes that keeping in touch with the needs of the community is an essential part of the organization's mission. Therefore, board members feel better qualified to determine individual grants based on their assessment of community needs. (See "What Is a Community Foundation?" in the Appendix.)

Identification by Gift Deductibility

The primary difference between private foundations and public charities involves the deductibility of gifts of appreciated assets. Specifically, there is a different approach to assigning a value to donations. A donor will receive a deduction for the full amount of a cash gift up to the amount he is permitted to contribute (based on a percentage of his income). In addition, a gift of qualified stock that has appreciated may offer the donor a market value deduction (also subject to income limitations). However, if someone donates highly appreciated stock (whether publicly traded or not), real estate, or any other type of appreciated asset to a 501(c)3 organization, the donor receives the current market value (which is usually a higher number) as his deduction rather than the price paid for the asset. For example, if an investor bought IBM stock in 1958 and gave it to a private foundation, he would only receive a deduction for its 1958 value, a small fraction of its current worth. If, however, he gave it to a public charity, his deduction would be the full current value of the stock.

Identifying Potential Donor Foundations

The reality is that a vast majority of the foundations making grants are relatively small, with only 100,000 to 10 million dollars in assets. They are generally required to give away five percent of their assets each year. For instance, a 100,000 dollar foundation will give away 5,000 a year; a one million dollar foundation, 50,000 a year; and a 10 million dollar foundation, 500,000 a year.

The Foundation Center Web site states that 61,810 foundations with 476.79 billion dollars in assets gave away 30.5 billion dollars in 2000. Their information comes from copies of the IRS Form 990PF filed by all private foundations. The center gets this information from the IRS in CD-ROM format. However, they obtain detailed financial and programmatic information from their own annual survey of more than 7,000 mid-sized and large foundations.[2]

Most of the small foundations (probably 49,000 or more) do not have a staff, and their grants go to organizations in which the grantor or the family of the grantor has an interest. Often, they do not even open letters of inquiry unless the letter is from someone they know. A number of directories and data sources, including the attorney general's office in each state, have a list of the foundations. Fund development staff should learn about the foundations in the service agency's geographic area, through a search by state or by metropolitan area. The next step involves finding out what currently funds a potential foundation and who knows the principals. If current volunteers or board members have no connections, staff can try to arrange a telephone conversation to invite the principals to visit or attend a social function the agency is hosting. If foundation personnel are only willing to look at materials, the development department can send the information and have a staff person follow up with a personal call to see if the material arrived and if the agency mission is one they are interested in supporting. In many cases, these foundations are already over-committed to the grantor's choice of organizations, but staying in touch and reminding them of the agency's programs and activities may eventually attract their attention.

The medium and large foundations with 10 to 500 million dollars in assets are usually focused on very specific geographic areas and interests. Many of these foundations have full-time staff people or consultants who assist the grantors or directors in reviewing grants. The development department can request the guidelines of the foundations in their region that have shown interest in supporting activities and programs similar to those of the service agency. Some foundations will not answer because they do not invite unsolicited inquiries and are already over-committed, while others will oblige. When a foundation responds, the development department staff should review the material and call the foundation to discuss projects and needs that coincide with both organizations' priorities. If foundation personnel show an interest in the agency's mission, it is wise to send a brief letter outlining the project for which the agency is requesting support, rather than dashing off a proposal.

Table 9.2

Giving by the Ten Largest U.S. Foundations for 2003

Foundation (State)	2002 Assets in Dollars
Bill and Melinda Gates Foundation (WA)	26,810,518,000
Lilly Endowment, Inc. (IN)	10,849,406,670
The Ford Foundation (NY)	10,015,612,595
J. Paul Getty Trust (CA)	8,623,795,970
The Robert Wood Johnson Foundation (NJ)	7,933,791,000
The David and Lucile Packard Foundation (CA)	5,982,168,233
W. K. Kellogg Foundation (MI)	5,729,303,302
The William and Flora Hewlett Foundation (CA)	5,144,254,523
The Andrew W. Mellon Foundation (NY)	4,719,646,000
John D. and Catherine T. MacArthur Foundation (IL)	3,836,621,632

Source: "Top 100 U.S. Foundations by Asset Size," The Foundation Center, http://fdncenter.org.[3]

According to Brad Wolverton, the 133 foundations that provided asset firgures to *The Chronicle of Philanthropy* were worth 149.8 billion dollars in 2002. The total assets of all of the (56,000) foundations in the United States were 486 billion dollars.[4] So, if 133 foundations have 149.8 billion dollars, the other 55,867 foundations share the remaining 347 billion dollars in assets.

It is interesting to note in the listing of the 138 major foundations that one of the smallest in assets is the Paul G. Allen Charitable Foundation in Seattle. While many foundations give away the minimum required, the Allen foundation is much more generous; it approved over 36 million in grants in 2002[5] and 120 million in donations and pledges in 2003.[6] Some individuals who start a foundation choose their area of interest and then fund that interest with additional donations of highly appreciated stock on an ongoing basis. So, the key to analyzing foundation giving is not only what the assets are, but how deep the pockets of the major donor are, and how much that person has been giving to fulfill his or her life mission.

In addition, the agency development department needs to answer four essential questions when approaching a philanthropic organization for support. They are:

- How closely does the organizational mission match the foundation's purpose?
- How can the agency's request be presented to that foundation most advantageously?
- Who in the agency's constituency has a connection to that foundation and its purpose?
- Who in the agency's circle of supporters knows the major donor?

It is also important to remember that at a community level, a foundation is often just an extension of one individual donor or corporate executive. For instance, if the name of one foundation located out of state keeps cropping up as a donor to local community efforts, it is highly likely that there is some tie to that particular community. People who are successful often remain loyal to their roots even when they move away.

Economic Factors

Economic trends notwithstanding, it is clear that foundations are a major force in nonprofit sector funding. Since the year 2000, the United States economy has seen some major downturns. Not surprisingly, foundations have been affected. Of the 138 major foundations with assets ranging from 100 million to 24 billion dollars, less than ten percent of them experienced an increase in asset value from 2002 to 2003. In other words, the experience of the major foundations is most likely to be reflected in smaller foundations. In fact, 90 percent of them have experienced a decline in assets due to the significant declines in the stock market and economy over the past few years. (Figures for the 100 largest foundations, adjusted annually, are available on The Foundation Center Web site: www.fdncenter.org/research/trends_analysis/top100assets.html.)

However, "in spite of three consecutive years of stock market declines and continuing weakness in the economy, giving by the nation's nearly 62,000 grant-making foundations remained steady in 2002 at an estimated 30.3 billion dollars, almost unchanged from 30.5 billion in 2001."[7]

10

CREATING A SUPPORT FOUNDATION AND ITS BOARD

Many 501(c)3 organizations have opted to create their own support foundations to raise money more effectively and manage hard assets. There are a number of reasons for this decision, including:

- To acquaint people with significant assets and influence in the community with the agency's needs
- To generate more dollars for the agency programs, capital needs, or the establishment of an endowment
- To augment the existing board members' ability and efforts in fund raising by attracting individuals and companies who have the capacity to make large gifts and influence others they know to do so as well.
* To complement the existing board members' time and talent by having people in a support organization who are truly knowledgeable about the management of significant assets and endowments so that informed policy decisions can be made and monitored
- To take advantage of the possible benefits of having a separate entity own assets and receive contributions (In some states, contributions are actually used to offset or reduce grant dollars and fee-for-service dollars.)
- To provide the type of management and accountability policies, and board member experience, necessary for service organizations that operate one or more businesses for profit (such as a resale shop, embroidery service or manufacturing concern).

Make all you can,
save all you can,
give all you can.

John Wesley

In each of these cases, a support foundation can define its mission as exclusively for the support of the agency. If the parent organization chooses to have a foundation address specific issues, it may do so. The usual functions are:

- Hold real estate and other real assets
- Hold and invest the funds for an endowment
- Hold and invest the funds for a capital campaign
- Own the businesses that provide employment opportunities for the clients it serves.

Foundations Qualifying for 501(c)3 Status

Support organizations have been around since the 1969 tax code changes. Of course, since that time, more variations of support organizations have developed. In fact, even individuals can choose to set up a support organization, provided that more than half the board members are independent (that is, not members of the individual's family or corporation).

The type of support foundation discussed here relies on the 501(c)3 status of the parent entity, a direct service organization that receives the majority of its operating funds through public money. (Public money includes grants funded by tax dollars or fees for service.) In addition, the support organization board is made up of a majority of members of the 501(c)3 organization. Therefore, it automatically qualifies for 501(c)3 status.

In the most conservative interpretation of the support foundation, the parent organization, a public charity, must control a majority of the board. For example, a nine-person board would include the public charity's executive director, chief financial officer, board president and two existing board members who fit the criteria for foundation directors. The remaining four positions would be filled by persons outside the service organization. Such a board is legally defined as controlled by a public charity. (The organiztion's legal and tax counsel can explain nuances and make recommendations about how the word "control" is defined.) With the board in place and the parent organization's dependence on public money established, the foundation can receive large private contributions from a few people without being classified as a private foundation.

Director and Trustee Qualifications

If one purpose of the foundation is to raise money and protect assets, the directors should be individuals of affluence and influence. In other words, they should have the ability to make large gifts themselves and influence other individuals in the community to do the same. Whether your organization's definition of a major gift is 10,000 dollars or 100,000 dollars, the candidates for the foundation board should have the capacity and willingness to contribute at that level.

At the power level of the community, everyone knows who can give at higher levels. For example, a leading clergyman may have no wealth in his own right but may know who does. The power structure consists of people who have affluence and/or influence. They tend to socialize with each other, talk about each other, know what companies they control, which country clubs they belong to, and whether or not they are charitably inclined. They also know enough personal history about the people in their social circle to determine, to some degree, whether a prospective donor might be interested in the service organization's cause. Even if they do not know each other personally, they often know someone who does and can set in motion the steps necessary to be introduced in an advantaged way.

Persons of influence are very important to the service agency. For instance, if the agency finds that it needs job placement opportunities for the individuals it serves, a simple phone call to a person of influence can resolve the issue quickly. He may be able to contact the executive of another organization and open employment opportunities in that company for the agency's clients. In another scenario, agency management may discover that a particular piece of legislation will threaten or benefit the organization or one of its programs. A person of influence can introduce agency representatives to a person or persons at the highest political levels and help the agency sway votes in its favor.

In addition to having affluence and influence, some candidates should be selected on the basis of their skills and knowledge. For example, if the foundation is responsible for investing and protecting the endowment funds, then at least one candidate should have experience in that area. She should have experience dealing with large personal investments, whether it was in a position of significant responsibility in an investment firm or on another board.

If one purpose of the foundation is responsibility for real estate assets–acquisition, maintenance and potential sale or exchange–then one foundation candidate should have significant affluence, influence and knowledge in the area of real estate. Again, that experience should include personal real estate holdings; a board member position with a real estate investment trust, another nonprofit organization or similar concern; or professional real estate management.

If one of the foundation's purposes is to expand businesses run by the service organization, one candidate should be a very successful entrepreneur in a business or businesses similar to those developed by the service agency. He should know how to make agency-associated businesses more profitable and market them more effectively.

The foundation board should also include an attorney. If the service organization has an attorney on its board, he would be a logical choice for one of the overlapping board members. The attorney would naturally be the person to draw up the necessary incorporation papers and conduct the appropriate filings with the IRS and the state.

Initiating the Foundation

The first step in establishing a foundation is to form a group or nominating committee that will identify prospects for the foundation board. The committee should include the executive director, the director of development (or other staff person responsible for the nongovernmental support of the organization), the president of the board and the fund-raising chair. The group then determines the process for submitting names of prospects. Usually, it starts with collecting biographical data and listing reasons for inviting each prospect to be a part of the board. The committee might also identify the best person to approach a potential board member to ask for a commitment.

During the prospect identification process, group members should keep in mind that they are inviting people to be "founding members" of an important organization. That distinction often attracts recruits. While some organizations already have experienced, affluent and influential individuals as part of their constituencies, many others do not. In this case, the committee must reach out further into the community. Recruiting becomes more complicated, but the process can be made more manageable by following a logical procedure. Once the most respected, influential and wealthy members of the community have been identified, the committee should single out the most approachable person among them. Next, the person making contact should explain the work of the agency, the needs that are still unmet, and why the prospect's involvement is necessary. Communicating openly and clearly is essential. As one fund-raising professional put it, "Be prepared to answer critical questions on your budget and management. Be scrupulously honest. Redefine why you need this specific person to help you recruit other influential people or 'substantial' members of the community."[1]

The prospect should be told exactly what is expected of him. For example, the recruiter might say, "Each foundation director is expected to give five to ten thousand dollars a year to the agency and will be responsible for raising 25 thousand a year." Agency management should supply accurate numbers for a financial commitment, and the committee should supply an accurate description of the time commitment. If recruiters use the "We only want to use your name" approach, they will attract people who expect to do nothing and give nothing.

> We need to be angels for each other, to give each other strength and consolation.
>
> Henri J. M. Nouwen

Once the director positions are filled, the committee can make trustee positions available to other individuals. A trustee might meet the criteria for becoming a foundation director, including an investment in helping the organization, but can only attend one meeting a year. These individuals would most likely be somewhat older; however, they would know the "movers and shakers" well enough that one call from them could bring great results. The trustee positions are also a method of maintaining important connections. For example, when foundation directors complete their terms, they can be graduated to a position on the board of trustees. This keeps them officially involved with the organization.

Members of the foundation board establish the times and frequency of their meetings. Some organizations run with monthly executive committee meetings and quarterly board meetings, often an effective and efficient use of members' time. Others decide that quarterly board meetings are sufficient.

The foundation should also have stationery designed specifically for its purposes. An essential element on the letterhead is a list of the directors and trustees. In addition, the design should include the executive director's office address and phone number.

As always, service organization management must remember that people give to organizations they care about and are involved in. The foundation is an excellent, long-term way to involve people who have the capacity to make larger gifts.

11
ORGANIZING A CAPITAL CAMPAIGN

Developing a capital campaign for the human service agency is a complex project that requires meticulous research and planning long before the first donations are sought. The CEO and the board should gain a full understanding of the steps necessary to carry out a successful campaign.

The CEO is generally the person who first identifies the need for capital expansion. He then presents the idea to the board, who must decide whether they want to embark on a capital campaign. If the desire is there, they need to prepare a clear expression of the need and make a commitment of both time and money to support the project.

If the organization has never conducted a capital campaign, or the board has questions about their ability to raise the amount of money needed, it might be wise to hire an outside fund raising, consulting firm to do an assessment of the service agency's readiness for a capital campaign. The assessment can also be done internally. It includes analysis of the organization's structure and purpose, donor giving patterns, the status of the database and the willingness of major donors to assume leadership roles. The degree of readiness for a campaign rests, to a large extent, on the agency's consistent efforts to keep good donor records and its ability to recruit sufficient volunteers and board members willing to invest time and energy into fund raising. A number of small organizations fail the evaluation because their historical records of voluntary giving are not adequate or their voluntary leadership is not

> The price
> of living is
> giving.
>
> Author unknown

strong in fund raising. If that is the case, then the first step is to start keeping good donor records and recruiting more.

Campaign Organizational Structure

When an organization has a strong board of directors who are individually committed to fund raising, a database that is in good working order, and a constituency of known donors that can give at a level to support the goal, the agency is ready to initiate a capital campaign. The CEO and the board begin the process by appointing a steering committee that sits down with a list of agency prospects who have given as well as prospective donors who could be approached. After meeting with prospects, the steering committee might recommend a specific campaign chairperson, or the board might decide on a specific individual.

Whether a chairperson is in place or not, the next step involves selecting a steering committee. The chairperson (if one has accepted the position), the CEO, the board and the director of development work together to select committee members who are acquainted with the organization and its people. The steering committee performs a variety of tasks. One is to consider the number of agency donors and volunteers based on information in the agency database. Another is to make recommendations about the need for outside fund-raising counsel. It also identifies who the best candidates for large gifts are, selects the top ten leading prospects, and assesses what other volunteer leadership is already available to help achieve the funding goal. If a chairperson has not been appointed, the steering committee chooses a candidate and presents the suggestion to the CEO and the board. The committee may get help with both selection and recruiting if an outside fund-raising counsel has been evaluating the organization.

The next step in the process is to identify the capital campaign committee members. The chair or co-chairs work with the steering committee and the board to draw on volunteers already available in the agency constituency, and then, to a lesser degree, new recruits. For instance, the chair may have worked with others in the community on successful campaigns and know an individual who might be willing to work on a new project. Relationships and past experience are always key to developing a successful working team.

Once the campaign committee is in place, the director of development can work with the board and the committee members to designate persons most likely to be successful in approaching each prospect for the top ten gifts. If the steering committee has done its homework (based on good data from the development department), and the agency board provides support in any way it can, the capital campaign committee's work should go smoothly.

Table 11.1

Sample Campaign Organizational Chart		
Chief Executive Officer and Board		
Campaign Chair		
Steering Committee (Prospect Rating)	Campaign Executive Committee	Development Staff
Major Gifts Committee	Special Gifts Committee	General Gifts Committee

Soliciting the Top Ten Gifts

The common lore in fund raising is that 40 to 50 percent of capital campaign funds must come from the top ten gifts. If not, the campaign will not succeed and must be downsized. Also, the 80/20 rule states that 80 percent of the gifts come from 20 percent of the donors. This is possible only for some organizations. For example, universities have offices for *advancement* to develop the contacts with people who are already giving and can increase their giving levels substantially. But, community agencies have offices for *development*, because they need to develop relationships with those people. A local agency with one donor who is capable of giving one million dollars considers itself fortunate, while universities see many donations of this size.

The need to concentrate on high-end donors can be discouraging for human service agencies that do not have affluent constituencies or communities. In an organization with only a few board members who are involved in fund raising, and a less-than-affluent constituency, the development director's role is elevated and the need for a support foundation increases. While adding affluent board members is an option, it is a time-consuming one that often cannot be accomplished before a new building must be built.

Fortunately, the need for capital for a building campaign can be a very cohesive force in developing a loyal constituency. Working together toward a tangible, realistic goal and achieving success can create a synergy that bonds everyone on the campaign to each other and to the organization. For example, everyone experiences tension when the steering committee finally names the organizations/individuals most likely to make the top ten gifts and the individuals who will solicit them. Seeing the dollar amount that is needed can be incredibly daunting. The tension remains if, after careful analysis of the first wave of efforts, the gap between the goal and the resources available is still great. It can be a searing experience for an organization that has not developed a following of people capable of making large gifts. Nonetheless, if each successful ask is celebrated and the mission remains clear, setbacks can be a motivating force for volunteers. They may renew their efforts to make contact with people they know and try to get them more involved.

When a campaign begins, enthusiasm weighs heavily, but after following the formula for generating 50 percent of the funds from the top ten gifts, reality sets in. In fact, most of the volunteers will choose to work on getting the second 50 percent first, because the gifts are for smaller amounts. It is therefore essential that the lead gifts are identified and committed before going public with the campaign.

Structuring Anticipated Gifts

The first 40 to 50 percent of a campaign goal of four million dollars is between one and 1.6 million dollars. When people suggest that they will achieve the goal by soliciting 400 gifts at 1,000 dollars each, they are not being realistic. One look at the demographics of the community often reveals that very few individuals can donate a sum that large. Indeed, a 100-dollar gift from one family could represent one percent of its after-tax income, while 10,000 represents a half percent of another family's after-tax income.

The following charts (Tables 11.2, 11.3, 11.4, and 11.5) provide examples of possible gifts, gift ranges, and the number of prospects that are needed to achieve campaign goals beginniing with one million dollars. Charts like these can help development staff and volunteers understand the people and dollars needed to accomplish their goals.

Table 11.2

Illustration of a Mathematically Developed Traditional Gifts Table–$1 Million Goal

Gift Type	Gift Range	Number of Gifts	Number of Prospects Needed	Total
Major gifts	$100,000	1	4	$100,000
	50,000	2	8	100,000
	25,000	4	16	100,000
Special gifts	12,500	8	24	100,000
	6,250	16	48	100,000
	3,125	32	96	100,000
	1,560	64	128	80,000
General gifts less than	1,500	many	many	320,000
				$1,000,000

Source: Dove, *Conducting a Successful Capital Campaign.*[1]

Table 11.3

Standards of Giving
Necessary for Success in a $2 Million Campaign

Gift Type	Gift Range	Number of Gifts	Total
Major gifts	$400,000	1	$400,000
	250,000	1	250,000
	150,000	1	150,000
	100,000	2	200,000
	50,000	2	100,000
Special gifts	25,000	10	250,000
	10,000	15	150,000
	5,000	25	125,000
General gifts less than	5,000	all other	375,000
			$2,000,000

Source: Dove, *Conducting a Successful Capital Campaign.*[2]

Table 11.4

**Standards of Giving
Necessary for Success in a $4 Million Campaign**

Gift Type	Gift Range	Number of Gifts	Total
Major gifts	$500,000	1	$500,000
	300,000	1	300,000
	200,000	2	400,000
	150,000	3	500,000
	100,000	5	500,000
Special gifts	50,000	10	600,000
	25,000	14	400,000
	15,000	25	375,000
General gifts less than	10,000	all others	425,000
			$4,000,000

Source: Dove, *Conducting a Successful Capital Campaign*.[3]

Table 11.5

	Standards of Giving **Necessary for Success in a $6 Million Campaign**		
Gift Type	*Gift Range*	*Number of Gifts*	*Total*
Major gifts	750,000	1	$750,000
	500,000	1	500,000
	300,000	3	850,000
	200,000	4	800,000
	150,000	4	700,000
	100,000	6	600,000
Special gifts	50,000	10	600,000
	25,000	14	400,000
	15,000	25	375,000
General gifts less than	10,000	all others	425,000
			$6,000,000

Source: Dove, *Conducting a Successful Capital Campaign*.[4]

An agency with virtually no possibility of getting a one million dollar gift or even several in the 400,000 and 250,000 dollar range from their community is particularly handicapped if it needs to raise four million dollars. It may succeed in reaching the funding goal by mixing state, county and federal grants along with private contributions. Table 11.6 below gives an example of such a donation/grant mix. The chart indicates that at least four warm or hot prospects are needed for a single gift at the upper ranges. When gifts are 15,000 dollars and below, a lower number of warm or hot prospects are needed per gift because a larger percentage of the general population is able to give in that category. It is also important to note that the agency could be receiving individual pledges paid over a period of three to five years.

The final average of 7,500 gifts at 100 dollars each indicates that the organization would need 8,000 donors to make this goal. That includes approximately 12 donors and 46 qualified prospects for the first set of gifts (1.9 million dollars), and 140 donors or 375 prospects for the second set of gifts (1.2 million dollars). The remaining gifts–more than 7,000 at an average of 100 dollars each–could possibly require as many as 22,500 prospects. In reality, those 7,500 gifts averaging 100 dollars each would be more likely to come from 2,500 to 3,000 donors at the rate of 100 dollars a year for three years. So, it is not as scary as the mathematical model would indicate.

Even so, it is clear that a database of 5,000 individual donors is the benchmark to achieve a four million dollar campaign. And, it is important to remember that even if the agency has a 5,000-person constituency, chances are not all of them are donors. Furthermore, without 200 plus donors who can make gifts of 10,000 to 250,000 dollars, it becomes even more essential to scour the agency for those two or three people who can each give one million dollars. This illustrates why making an honest, realistic evaluation of donor giving power is so important, and why the real key to achieving a campaign goal is quality leadership.

Table 11.6

Human Service Agency Campaign for $4,000,000

Gift Type	Gift Range	Number of Gifts	Number of Prospects	Total
State Grant	$1,000,000	1	4	$1,000,000
Private Donor	$250,000	1	4	250,000
Private Donor	$200,000	1	4	200,000
Federal Grant	$150,000	1	3	150,000
Private Donor	$100,000	2	8	200,000
Private Donor	$75,000	2	8	150,000
County Grant	$50,000	1	3	50,000
Private Donor	$50,000	3	12	150,000
Special Gifts	$25,000	10	40	250,000
Private Donor	$15,000	20	60	300,000
	$10,00	40	100	400,000
	$5,000	40	100	150,000
	$3000	30	75	90,000
General Gifts less than	$2500	Many	Many, many	750,000

Average 7,500 gifts @$100

Recruiting Volunteers and Staff

As mentioned earlier, the top leaders of the capital campaign should be highly visible, influential individuals in the community. While they are crucial to the project, they are also very busy people who should only be used to do things that are vital to the success of the project. So, selecting the campaign chair and staffing his committee should be carried out thoughtfully. The board chair and the CEO should approach the potential campaign leader personally. (Again, the campaign chair should be someone who is well respected and visible in the community, and cares about the organization and has a track record of giving and motivating others to give.) When the candidate decides to accept, he may also want the board chair and/or the CEO to extend the same courtesy to prospective members of the committee.

Asking people to commit to voluntary projects is a very sensitive task. Every factor that can be employed to get a positive commitment should be used. If a person is more apt to say "yes" to one individual than another, the decision about who will make contact is obvious. While individuals take on projects because they want to help a favored cause, it is also true that people respond to other people. However, if the request is for someone to fill a leadership position, then only top leaders should be doing the asking.

Of course, the dynamics of each organization are different. Agency personnel acquainted with its culture will know best which combination of formal and volunteer leadership should be asking prospective volunteers to help. The goal is to get a positive response as often as possible so the campaign can be staffed with the most competent people in the community.

The campaign chair also recruits volunteers. He should always ask the second tier of volunteers by letter. Since he may not know that some of these people are already involved in the organization, it is perfectly appropriate for them to receive a formal letter from the chair. Once the letter has gone out, a member of the capital campaign committee or the development staff can also contact the prospects. The message might be, "You're going to get a letter from Mr. Boyd. We're really excited to have him leading the capital campaign, and we hope you'll seriously consider getting involved." The contact person might also explain briefly why the leader is such an asset to the campaign, and answer the prospect's questions. That helps build excitement and willingness to serve on a project that has all the earmarks of being successful.

Volunteer Assignments

The efficient supervision of volunteers is an important key to success in any campaign. The agency staff must coordinate volunteer assignments since they have access to details of the campaign plan. They should also furnish technical know-how, supply mechanical and clerical support, provide resource information and keep records. Encouraging and energizing the volunteers is another aspect of the job. The volunteers are, after all, at the center of the activity–and in the spotlight–because their dedication enables the agency to achieve its funding goals.

First, agency staff should show consideration for the volunteers' time. In order to do this efficiently, staff members must assess what type of volunteer assistance is needed. As previously stated, the most important jobs are asking for donations and recruiting new volunteers and prospective donors. But, other jobs, such as calling people on the list, addressing envelopes, mailing post cards, and assembling information for follow up mailings, are essential. Knowing what positions need to be filled, staff members can assign responsibilities according to the talents and wishes of those available. In addition, staff members should be very clear about the duties required by the assignment and provide training in each area when necessary.

Training is most important for volunteers who are appealing for donations. They need to feel comfortable with what they are saying when they begin calling prospective donors. A training session that includes role-playing is often a very good technique. Volunteers should play the role of both the caller and the prospective donor. This exercise allows them to test their own commitment as they gain confidence in their own ability to ask for a contribution. (These role plays are real. Each volunteer is asking another how much he or she plans to give.) Of course, some of the volunteers will already have experience with the job, and can probably take the lead during training sessions. They can demonstrate how they like to approach the donation appeal–following the script prepared by the development or campaign staff while adding their personal style.

Some volunteers are not willing to ask directly for contributions but are comfortable inviting their friends to a campaign meeting or luncheon where the campaign chair explains the need for contributions and volunteers. Other people like to work in groups, and still others are individual achievers. The whole fund-raising process is about selecting an objective and creating an environment that encourages each individual to do what he does best to achieve a specific goal.

Regular committee progress reports can be a strong motivating force. When volunteers are provided with the names of firm commitments from individuals and organizations, they are able to track their achievements. not only does the individual get a boost, but volunteers encourage each other as they see the headway they have made over time. Detailed campaign reports should also go to the executive committee and to each subcommittee chair. Summary reports should be shared with the whole committee to the extent that it is possible. A spirit of friendly competition can emerge and may well be encouraged. Sometimes, competition may create personality conflicts between volunteers or between staff members and volunteers. Committee chairs or supervisors should use conflict resolution methods appropriate to the situation and help personnel focus on the job at hand.

> Love
> is a fruit
> in season
> at all times.
>
> Mother Teresa

People in the helping professions are proficient at aiding people who face special challenges. So naturally, many of them should also enjoy helping volunteers develop a sense of fulfillment as they use their unique talents on the project. Volunteers should also enjoy and value staff assistance. With proper leadership, it can and should be a truly positive experience for everyone.

Naming Opportunities

As the project is solidified and architectural plans completed, a series of naming opportunities should be identified, with price tags attached to each. The building itself is usually one naming opportunity. Depending on the other unique spaces in the building, naming opportunities can be matched with possible donors. For example, a gym might attract the interest of a prominent athlete or a company involved in sports. An amateur who loves sports or fitness might also value the opportunity to have such a facility named for his family. A kitchen and dining space could provide an opportunity for a food company, a successful family in the restaurant business or a wealthy individual who enjoys dining. The large lobby or auditorium, used frequently by large numbers of people, is especially appealing to corporate donors concerned with name visibility. In addition, individual classrooms and training or counseling areas can each have a name attached. The rooms are very meaningful to persons who feel that the essence of the program they love is alive in these spaces.

As much as people laugh at the concept of "edifice complex," capital gifts remain more appealing than annual gifts because they fund projects that are expected to last. Bricks and mortar tend to symbolize permanence, and leaving a lasting legacy is a great desire for many philanthropic individuals.

It is wise to construct a gift table as well as a list of giving or naming opportunities during the campaign. While some individuals are adamant about wanting their gift to be anonymous, they usually want to know what the money is used for. Other individuals want recognition and like to have prominent, naming opportunities. Many people just want the gratification of seeing their name connected to a project that they believe in and helped create.

Table 11.7 gives examples of naming options for a capital campaign. Each space does not necessarily need a price that corresponds exactly to the amount of space occupied or to the exact construction cost. Clearly, each building is unique, so agency administrators and campaign personnel can assign prices to spaces based on their function, relative importance and size. The main goal is to provide one more motivational link for donors to connect to the project.

Table 11.7

Naming Opportunities for a $4 Million Capital Campaign

Space to Name	Price	Number of Opportunities
Naming of building	$1,000,000	1
Auditorium	300,000	1
Road to entry if private drive	250,000	1
Entry portico or lobby	200,000	1
Exercise room	100,000	1
Computer equipment	100,000	
Kitchen	100,000	1
Cafeteria or dining room	100,000	1
Individual therapy rooms	50,000	5
Outdoor playing fields	50,000	2
Individual classrooms	50,000	5
Individual program space	50,000	5
Specialized educational equipment	5,000 to 50,000	10
Administrative offices	50,000	1
Therapist offices	5,000 each	10
Psychiatrist office	10,000	1
Psychologists offices	10,000 each	3
Counselors offices	5,000 each	5
Outdoor garden benches (each)	2,000	10
Paver bricks for patio	100 each	1,000

The Campaign Timetable

Campaign timetables vary with the size of the human service agency, the project and its constituency. Everyone concerned with the campaign should understand that it is almost always a long and time-consuming proposition. A campaign in three phases can be divided into the following series of steps. Laying out the phases and the targeted time frame for everyone to see allows agency administrators and staff to track both the duties and the time required for capital campaigns.

Phase 1: Before the Public Announcement (12 to 24 months)

- Develop a clear mission statement for the organization.
- Create a strategic plan for the development of the organization.
- Develop a clear statement of the organizational structure of the 501(c)3 non-profit.
- Develop the statement of need for the capital campaign.
- Bring in outside counsel if necessary to evaluate the agency donor resources and record keeping systems.
- Hire needed staff and bring the database up to date. Buy new software if the system does not keep the appropriate type of records.
- Do a data transfer from old software (if needed) or reenter old data to bring the system up to date.
- Select a steering committee.
- Identify individual prospects for the top 20 gifts.
- Select the campaign leadership.
- Design the campaign structure, including a gift table with naming opportunities.
- Develop and publish the campaign materials.
- Recruit and train a major gift committee.
- Seek lead gifts.
- Recruit and train special gift committees.
- Seek special gifts.
- Recruit a general gifts committee chairperson.
- To end the first phase, announce the campaign.

The announcement is generally made when donors have pledged a minimum of 30 percent of the campaign goal. (Many agencies wait until they have collected 50 percent of the funds in cash and pledges before they make the public campaign announcement.) Also, the more up to date the database and the stronger the giving constituency, the less time is needed to gear up for a capital campaign. If the database needs work and volunteers and donors need to be recruited, the first phase can take up to two years.

Phase 2: The Public Campaign (18 to 24 months)
- Continue seeking major gifts and special gifts.
- Add more members to the major gifts and special gifts committees.
- Recruit and train volunteers for the general gifts committee.
- Begin the general gifts (grassroots) campaign.
- Continue refining campaign literature.
- Seek ongoing major media coverage of all areas of the campaign.
- Keep a regular schedule of meetings with volunteers.
- Close the second phase when 80 percent of the goal is reached.

Phase 3: The Campaign Conclusion (12 months)
- Focus the general gifts or grassroots campaign on reaching the final 20 percent of the goal.
- Be prepared for additional major gifts or increases on some pledges.
- Celebrate the victory!

This timetable can represent two to four years of work, and it is necessary to create a sense of urgency for the campaign to succeed. If realistic timetables are not established and met, the campaign loses momentum and becomes a continual, slow-moving effort to reach a seemingly unattainable goal.

The special gifts category generally includes donations from clubs and other organizations such as unions and fraternal orders. Those gifts are almost mini campaigns within each organization. Naming opportunities in these situations are a big issue because The Rotary Club of Elmhurst or the Lions Club of Springfield will enjoy seeing their names on a classroom or therapy room long after the members who raised the money are no longer part of the club.

Unions are a particularly good source for these gifts. Family members in the service agency who may not be able to make large gifts may belong to unions and can approach the union leadership. When appropriate, the service agency can arrange a tour of agency programs and facilities. Another possibility is to arrange a time to speak to them as groups, armed with audiovisual presentations of the agency's work and mission. The presenter should also explain the benefits that the new capital improvements would provide for the program(s).

Using the Database

Most literature about fund raising and capital campaigns relates to college or university alumni associations. Institutions that run fiftieth year reunions every year know the cost of such an event can be underwritten by the returning alumni who plan the event with staff and get back in touch with chums they have not seen for many years. That is possible because one person knows where somebody else is currently living. Consequently, a different set of alumni is "refreshed" every year and re-inspired to support their alma mater. Furthermore, the database remains current through the efforts of the alumni.

While human service agencies might have more difficulty getting help to keep their databases current because their alumni must deal with disabling conditions, building an accurate database for the entire organization remains an important issue. Theoretically, once software for client and fund-raising lists has been installed and the information entered, it is kept up to date. But, keeping it current can be very tedious. Tracking donors, alumni, clients and families along with addressing their privacy issues with appropriate security controls is always time-consuming though very important.

A capital campaign is often the impetus for updating. The development department can cut the time it expends by printing the donor list and assigning several volunteers to help staff members review it. They can provide the latest information on name changes, addresses and status, thus eliminating duplications. For instance, Mrs. Jones may be in the list six times because she sent donations in a variety of ways. She could be listed as Mrs. Pamela Jones, Mr. and Mrs. James E. Jones, Mr. and Mrs. James Jones, Mr. James Jones, the Jones Family Foundation, the Evergreen Plumbing Company, and the Jones Trust. Obviously, integrating the fund-raising lists into the general database is ideal. This prevents money from being wasted on duplicate mailing to the same person.

Maintaining a Relationship with Donors

Each service agency needs to develop its own system of keeping in touch with the alumni and families who have been served by the organization, whether or not they have made contributions in the past. Agencies that serve a large number of people who have no family ties, or whose families simply never become involved, have the most difficulty. However, a good number of alumni and families want to continue to help an agency that has provided them with so many essential services.

The best method is to ensure that the executive director and the development staff know that all the alumni and donors are listed in a completely current database. But, unless the database is reviewed annually and carefully, the organization will not come close to the ideal.

Furthermore, if the fund-raising officer and staff are relatively new, they will not know many of the past contributors, especially if they do not attend special events or volunteer in the program. In some instances, a check may arrive from a regular contributor, and no one in the office knows who the person is.

The single best way to update the database and connect with donors is to break the list down into smaller units and distribute them among the fund-raising or public relations staff and volunteers. They should then mail postcards to a number of people each week during the beginning stages of the campaign and call them the following week. If the donor constituency is small, the vast burden of the "making friends" activity will most likely fall on the fund-raising staff initially.

Each development person can call ten people who are already listed in the database as prospective donors a day. As time progresses, staff members or volunteers will follow up each day on five old prospects as well. These are people who were not available at the time of the call or who did not return a call.

The director of development must first cultivate relationships with the people who have given in the past and, second, start developing new prospects for donors and volunteers. Encouraging the existing volunteer constituency to contact additional future donors is key, and making that happen is a function of the "activity level" of the staff. Activity means initiating calls, making appointments and talking with people face to face. In the financial service business, that is what leads to sales. In fund raising, that is what leads to contributions.

Prospecting for Donors

The process of prospecting for donors should start with mailing a simple introductory piece every week to 50 individuals per prospector. The piece can be a postcard that briefly explains the new project, the need for the prospect's involvement, and the name of the person who will be calling. The postcard might state: "The ABC Foundation has a wonderful new project we would like to tell you about. Next week, Francis Green will be calling to talk to you about our exciting news."

Each individual then personally calls ten of the listed people each day for five days. The caller can expect to reach five people and get two or three appointments out of each ten phone calls to warm prospects (those who have given but to whom the prospector has never spoken). And the prospector can expect to reach three people and get at least one appointment out of each ten phone calls to cold prospects (those who have never given and were referred by someone or who may have some slight connection to the organization). Hot prospects (people who are actively interested in the organization and give regularly) are naturally more responsive. The prospector should be able to reach six or seven people and get three to four appointments out of every ten calls.

In addition to following up on persons who did not answer or return calls the week before, the prospector must follow up on incorrect and changed telephone numbers. In addition, returned mail requires research to locate the person. Generally, a clerk or other volunteer can be assigned to track down and correct the proper information so that errors in the database are further reduced.

A successful capital campaign should be well-structured and conducted with a sense of urgency. The best way to achieve results is to outline a specific time frame for each project. Table 11.8 shows a simple schedule for the development department and its volunteers.

Table 11.8

Sample Daily Staff Schedule

9 to 10 a.m. - Telephoning

10 to 11 a.m. - Staff meeting or volunteer meeting

11 to 12 noon - Letter and proposal writing

12 noon to 2 p.m. - Lunch with individual prospects/volunteers or both

2 to 3 p.m. - Returning phone calls, and finishing letters and proposals

3 to 4 p.m. - Appointment

4 to 5 p.m. - Appointment

Evening meeting - at least two or three times a week during the campaign

Realistically, unless some very strong volunteers are willing to work on this project, the burden of organizing and follow-up on the calling program falls on the development staff. Staff should check on volunteers each week to compare their progress to the campaign objectives. When a prospector has done as much as possible with the first 50 cards, staff can assign another 50. It is important to allow some time in the schedule for volunteers to call people they know who do not appear on the list. The best source of potential donors is people who have been referred by others, so this is the area where volunteers can be most helpful. In addition, the database may contain suppliers, professionals and other organizations with similar missions. Suppliers represent a particularly good source of potential donations. They should be approached by the staff unless an individual volunteer has a strong relationship with the supplier.

The development department may wish to use the phone bank concept, with several volunteers in the office one or two evenings a week making calls. Some people enjoy the camaraderie of this approach, and if the office arrangement lends itself to this system, it can be especially helpful with the initial phone calls. Giving volunteers the opportunity to hear each other on calls is reinforcing and helps them become more proficient with their own scripts. With this system, the volunteer follow-up calls are done at home.

Updating the Donor List

Cleaning up the mailing list is a very labor intensive process that should be done regularly but must be done for a capital campaign. Most organizations still have people in their database who donated or volunteered years ago but have not been active for some time. Again, the staff and volunteers must pool their knowledge about each individual, business or club, so they can re-contact as many as possible. For this reason, the development department may want to sort the list into current and past donors. It is usually easiest to track people who were involved in the most recent special events, or who donated in the past year or two.

If there is a problem with an entry in the database, there is more than one way to track down a current address or phone number. The entry may contain the name of the volunteer or staff person who originally brought an individual into the organization donor base. Ideally, that person would have new contact information and could be the one to make the initial call about the organization's current financial need. He could also indicate that someone from the agency fund-raising staff would like to have the opportunity for a personal visit.

Social service agencies have a different problem from colleges and hospitals that have large cadres of donors. They are not bound by the common wisdom that says, "Don't even call anyone who has contributed less than 100 dollars." In fact, the minimum contribution category in an agency's mailing campaign often is 100 dollars. So, even the regular 25-dollar donors may be good prospects for larger donations. Furthermore, the organization frequently does not have the luxury of relegating their 100-dollar and below donors to merely an annual or semi-annual mail campaign. For the small or mid-sized agency, these donors are golden.

Scripting Staff and Volunteer Calls

It is important that the prospectors feel their mission is to make and keep friends for the organization. The purpose of each phone call is to improve the relationship between the organization and the donor or prospect. If the prospect has never given before, the mission of the prospector is to make friends. If the donor has given, the call should acknowledge his past support and keep the relationship warm. So, the scripts should encourage positive interaction, provide specific information and prompt accurate responses.

> Kind people make
> the world
> a better place.
> Are you one of them?
> Good! I thought so.
> I can tell by your face!
>
> Vera Waters

Usually people are delighted to hear a friendly voice saying, "Thank you so much for helping us in the past! And we just wanted to update you on our current project. Would you like to come to an open house or have a personal tour of the agency? Or, would you prefer that I come to visit you?" After the prospective donor's response, the volunteer should immediately mention a specific time. For example, "Would Tuesday or Thursday morning be better for you?" It is the most effective way to get an appointment.

Table 11.9

Expected Results from Telephone Activity			
	Cold Prospects	*Warm Prospects*	*Hot Prospects*
Call	50	50	50
Contact	15	25	40
Appointments	5	10	20

The Heritage Society

When planned giving is part of a capital campaign, it allows people to include the organization in their estate planning. A heritage society is one vehicle organizations use to guide estate planning and preserve the organization for future generations. Since the early part of the twenty-first century is seeing a vast increase in the elderly population, it makes sense to have a heritage society built into the organizational plan. A donor's planned giving and final gifts can contribute greatly toward achieving the capital campaign goals. (See Chapter 12.)

12

DEVELOPING PLANNED GIVING

Fund raising is all about allocating resources to raise money for current needs. Planned giving allows philanthropic individuals to allocate their resources for future gifts or bequests to support the causes they believe in. Simple enough; however, assigning one's current, limited resources for future gifts is often a thorny issue. And the agency's pressing need for current contributions often keeps it from assigning resources to work on the potentially larger gifts that could be forthcoming. Ultimately, planned giving is a worthwhile investment for both parties.

> The real question
> is not
> how can I help,
> but how can I serve.
>
> Rachel Naomi Remen

Giving USA 2003 indicates that of the 240.92 billion dollars given in the year 2002, approximately 7.5 percent came from bequests.[1] This type of giving stems from estate planning, which, of course, comes from individuals. However, it may involve succession issues in privately and publicly held companies, or it may involve having a portion of the estate flow into a family foundation.

The largest voluntary gifts an agency will ever receive will be most likely in the form of a bequest. These gifts are usually certain but the timing of them is not; although death is definite, the time of death never is. The service agency interested in receiving these gifts must ask for them and plan in advance. That involves identifying who is interested in the organization and who has the ability to make a bequest. Remarkably, the answer is *everyone*-if he or she is so inclined, and if the service agency helps him take the appropriate steps.

In 1999, researchers at Boston College's Social Welfare Research Institute (SWRI) first estimated that 41 trillion dollars would be transferred via estates over the next 50 years.[2] In 2003, they reaffirmed that those figures were still valid.[3]

In an article in the *Journal of Gift Planning*, the researchers, Paul Schervish and John Havens addressed two erroneous assumptions made by critics: 1) that the entire transfer of wealth was going to heirs, and 2) that boomers would be the sole recipients. Schervish and Havens made it clear that the "wealth transfer" they described in their original report was not synonymous with "inheritance." In fact, they pointed out that "only $25 trillion of the $41 trillion transfer will pass from decedents' estates to their heirs. The remaining $17 trillion will go to estate taxes, charitable bequests, and estate settlement expenses."[4]

To those who assumed boomers to be the only recipients, the researchers further emphasized the 55-year time span (1998-2052) they had used in their study. They noted that while 25 trillion dollars was going to heirs, boomers might inherit 7.2 trillion dollars, "but the majority of the inheritance will be transferred to subsequent generations, including the children and grandchildren of the boomers. As the boomer generation ages and dies during the 55-year period, their role in the wealth transfer process will be the greater as benefactors than as beneficiaries."[5]

The 41-trillion-dollar estimate is based on every dime of the final combined estates of the entire 1998 adult population. Havens and Schervish also estimated how those assets would be divided. Of a total of six trillion dollars in charitable bequests, 24.6 trillion is expected to go to heirs, 8.5 trillion to estate taxes and 1.6 trillion to estate fees.[6] Obviously, six trillion in bequests is a big enough potential source of revenue over the next 50 years to give serious thought to starting a planned giving program.

The Havens-Schervish report offers other very interesting information, including a description of all of the challenges that these assumptions and predictions have prompted. (The report is available online at www.bc.edu/research/swri or Paul Schervish.)

The simplest way to start a planned giving program is to put an announcement in the service agency's newsletter asking the constituents to remember the organization in their wills. A memorial gifts program is a natural lead-in to planned giving because it connects the concept of being remembered with the service agency.

Establishing the Board's Planned Giving Policy

The agency must establish a board policy for the planned giving program and keep simple forms available for people who indicate an interest. As with any fund-raising campaign, every member of the board should lead the way. For example, if the agency wants the general public to include it in their wills, each board member can be asked to fill out a questionnaire about his own estate planning. Questions might include:

- Do you have a will?
- Do you have a living trust?
- Is the service agency that you serve included in your will?
- Do you have a life insurance policy that is basically paid up which you no longer need?
- Would it make sense to gift it to the charity and take a tax deduction?

Creating a Planned Giving Committee

The service agency should set up a planned giving committee of volunteers who can lend expertise and talk about the program in the community. Agency personnel should consider recruiting professionals who have specific expertise in estate planning–an attorney, a certified public accountant (CPA), a (certified and/or chartered) financial planner, a family wealth counselor and an investment banker. They should also include a few other individuals who are interested in achieving the organization's goals. Other professionals who are knowledgeable in this field include certain financial advisors, estate planners and planned giving specialists.

Organizing a Legacy Society (Heritage Society)

The agency development department should start a heritage or legacy society and make the first 100 people who sign up founding members. Meetings should be scheduled at least four times a year with good speakers who either can talk about aspects of estate planning or be inspirational–for instance, inviting people who have already included charity in their estate plan to consider including the agency. Speakers might include an attorney who can describe wills and trusts, a specialist in charitable remainder trusts, and a person knowledgeable about special needs trusts. (Special needs trusts will especially interest the parents of disabled family members.) At least, once a year, the CEO should give an update on the organization's achievements and goals. If there is a community foundation in the area, the agency could invite the foundation CEO to speak about the advantages of including the community foundation in one's estate plan, and what options are currently available. Some donors will feel more confident funneling money to the agency through such a foundation, especially if it has a longer history or higher profile than the agency.

> The excellence
> of a gift lies
> in the appropriateness
> rather than
> in its value.
>
> Charles Dudley Warner

The heritage or legacy society meetings are also a way to bring people up to date on agency projects and programs. They keep people involved and aware of opportunities to help. The gathering should be social in nature, with the planned giving staff and one or two committee members acting as host. Refreshments should be included after the meeting to enhance the opportunity to socialize.

The people most interested in the society will likely be those who are over 55, because it is at that time of life that they really confront their own mortality and start thinking about what is important. They are the ones who will be asking, "What will people remember me for?"

A significant national movement called Leave a Legacy can also help. Many banks, trust departments, attorneys, financial planners, accountants and others in allied fields are involved in helping people identify what is most important in their lives and how they want to be remembered. The legacy they help a person define might reflect a set of values, a way of life or a philosophy of living. Once defined, the intended legacy guides their decisions about distributing their material wealth during their lifetime and after.

Staffing the Planned Giving Program

The planned giving program should be an integrated effort, staffed with at least one part-time person. It is preferable to have a full-time person, but when resources are scarce, it is difficult to justify expenditures for staff that may not result in income for several years.

The ideal person is one who lives in the community and knows people of substance. His or her background should include fund raising and some level of financial planning. Age is also important. A person 50 or older is preferable, since he or she is most apt to know others in the same age group and be able to relate to issues that are common to them.

For a more detailed approach to starting a successful planned giving program, readers may wish to consult, ***Planned Giving for Social Service Agencies*** (High Tide Press, 2002).

SOCIAL VENTURE PHILANTHROPY

Social venture philanthropy is a unique and still-evolving form of fund raising. The term ***venture capital philanthropy*** seems to have first appeared in the 1984 annual report of the Peninsula Community Foundation (www.pcf.org). A few years later, the concept was popularized in the ***Harvard Business Review*** with the article titled "Virtuous Capital: What Foundations Can Learn from Venture Capitalists."

The critical difference between social venture philanthropists and many charitable donors is that they require measurable outcomes from their donations as though it were a stock investment. It is much the same strategy used by very large foundations and some government grants. In fact, these very specific expectations and the very personal involvement of the partners are what distinguish philanthropy from charitable giving.

> Sacrifice is giving up something good for something better.
>
> Author unknown

In current practice, this model of philanthropy applies six key elements:

- Investments in long-term business plans
- A managing partner relationship
- An accountability for results process
- Provision of cash and expertise
- An exit strategy.

Social venture partners (SVPs) differ from typical foundations or major charitable donors in several ways. Typically, a family foundation is funded by a senior family member who achieved wealth over a significant period of time, and who articulates the purpose of the organization. In most cases, these individuals have been involved with a variety of charitable causes through giving and serving on a number of boards.

SVPs, on the other hand, are usually organized as part of a community foundation. They are composed of groups of young people who achieved significant wealth at a very early age, often in the high tech industry. Because of their youth and total absorption in very successful but demanding businesses, they have found little time to become familiar with philanthropy. SVPs provide a means to educate them about how philanthropy works, how nonprofits function, and how to examine the needs of such organizations thoroughly. The partnerships offer them an opportunity to use their own talents to help improve the organizations and to meet other successful young people who share their interests. (See "Silicon Valley Social Venture Fund [SV2].")

While the typical foundation is operated by a single individual or family, SVPs hope to achieve a greater impact than they could individually by pooling their contributions and talents. The partners offer the nonprofit organization (investee) a specific amount of financial support for an identified project with specific outcomes. They also offer their individual talents, skills and time to help achieve the outcomes. If the nonprofit needs skills that the original partners do not have, the lead partner recruits others to provide them on a pro bono basis.

Just as individuals serve as volunteers on boards and committees of nonprofit organizations, SVP partners learn to lead and use their talents to help the organization achieve its goals more effectively. In fact, some of the early SVPs assumed that they could apply to the nonprofit sector the skills they had learned in growing their own organizations with venture capital money. They found that the task was not as easy as they had initially assumed.

Large and small foundations with individual grantors frequently place a time limit on the funds they offer for support. As a result, the 501(c)3 recipient must provide a strategy to replace the funds, specifying other funding or revenue sources that it will qualify for at the end of the three- to five-year period. SVPs require a similar exit strategy. Since they are modeled after venture capitalists, the funding commitment is for two to five years. Benchmark achievements along the way allow the nonprofit to keep each year's funding for that time period.

A venture capitalist expects an IPO, publicly sold stock and the return of his capital plus a handsome profit. The SVP partner's profit was once expected to be the fulfillment of measurable self-sustainability and organizational capacity, enabling both the organization and the SVP to move on to another challenge. However, it has been the experience of a number of SVPs that public funding challenges made self sustainability impossible, even though a number of the organizations they invested in did increase their organizational capacity. As a result, many SVPs eventually join the boards of the organizations they have stimulated with their investment and time, while others go on to help other nonprofits.

Another reality of this approach is that some nonprofits like to get the money but do not enjoy the hands-on involvement of the SVPs. The nonprofit must be open to scrutiny and recommendations on how to be more effective in the targeted areas.

Developing Organizational Strength

Many nonprofit organizations struggle with poorly qualified and underpaid executives as well as less than perfect operational systems. And unfortunately, they do so in service to some of the most vulnerable people in our society. In addition, staff burnout is often a major problem; innovation is difficult to sustain; and ongoing funding for educational and social service programs is consistently at risk for cuts. Furthermore, the boards of these organizations are often people who do not have pockets deep enough to allow them to subsidize the cuts themselves. The result is that enormous emphasis is placed on limiting administrative expenses so a majority of funds can go for program operation. Unfortunately, this can become a self-defeating cycle. Channeling money to programs is admirable, but funds should also be available for staff recruitment, training, innovation, systems for keeping records and tracking progress, and other essential management functions. Without them, the agency may hold its own but will eventually stagnate and the quality of services will deteriorate.

This short-sighted approach is often combined with another self-defeating leadership strategy. Letts, Ryan and Grossman summed it up succinctly, stating that many nonprofit organizations "have been conditioned by the existing grant seeking process to camouflage their organizational expenses and needs. Nonprofits need to begin articulating compelling organizational strategies and asking foundations to invest in those strategies."[1]

A better strategy is to present those weaknesses to potential donors along with a credible solution. Specifically, the agency should "articulate a disciplined plan for using the non-program money and show how that money will enhance the impact of programs."[2] They must also explain that they know what it will take to strengthen the organization and how to use resources efficiently to meet that challenge.[3]

> Give what you have.
> To someone,
> it may be better
> than you dare to think.
>
> Henry Wadsworth
> Longfellow

The social venture partnership model actually offers one of the solutions to the problems of funding and administrative costs. It brings to the table not only the money but a group of people who were successful because of their talents, and they offer those assets to help build organizational strength as well as provide program support when appropriate.

In 2003, Ben Gose stated that "venture philanthropy was all the rage during the technology boom. It went through a transformation after the market bust, but its ideals live on. . . . Some grant makers consider venture philanthropy mere marketing hype, but many nonprofit groups that have worked with venture funds say the advice and aid in strategic planning that they have received goes well beyond the support that they have gotten from traditional foundations."[4]

Phil Buchanan, executive director of the Center for Effective Philanthropy, believes that there is now better understanding and better communication between peope involved in venture philanthropy and those involved in more traditional philanthropy and charitable giving. "We're out of that strange period," he says, "where there was a sense that business was king and that the answer to every nonprofit problem was a market solution."[5]

Successful Social Venture Partnerships

In the late 1990s, proponents of "venture philanthropy" vowed that it would revolutionize the charitable world. However, many venture philanthropy funds did not last long enough to finance even a two-year program because the new dot-com start-up companies that provided revenue collapsed, and in some cases the stock was valueless.

Nonetheless, a number of funds have pulled through and continue to be effective. For example, Social Venture Partners International Affiliates is affiliated with a number of SVPs. They include SVPs in several cities—Austin, San Francisco, Boston, Cleveland, Dallas, Denver, Pittsburgh, Portland, San Diego, St. Louis—as well as Arizona, Delaware, British Columbia, Minnesota and Boulder County, Colorado. Seattle had the most with 270 partners, 38 investees and over seven million dollars in investments over the five years of their existence. (Listing as of August 3, 2004.) Early stage SVPs include Chicago, Houston, Los Angeles, New Mexico, Rhode Island and Baja, Mexico.[6] Table 13.1 gives the specifics on those SVPs.

Another SVP called Venture Philanthropy Partners focuses on helping children from low-income families in and around Washington, D.C. The fund raised 30 million dollars—twice its goal—despite incorporating in 2000 just before the stock market slide.[7] Another successful SVP is the New Schools Venture Fund in San Francisco. It focuses on improving elementary and secondary education. The partnership created more than 1,200 small high schools in different parts of the county with investments of over 475 million dollars in just three years. The Bill and Melinda Gates Foundation has pledged 22 million dollars, the effort's largest grant so far.[8]

Recently, Ron Gother, a personal estate planning attorney for Walt Disney, began volunteering his time as president of the newly formed Desert Community Foundation. He was joined by Lothar Vascholtz, a retired insurance company executive who has assiduously researched SVP organizations. The two held a meeting of community leaders in the Coachella Valley of California to explore the possibility of starting SVPs in that area. Alan Sorkin, who spearheaded the

San Diego SVP, was one of the speakers. That SVP had invested approximately 500,000 dollars in local organizations over the previous three years. A few responders said that the donated time was at least double the amount of money received and one said "priceless."[9] Despite these obvious success stories, the Desert Community Foundation eventually determined that SVPs were currently not feasible in their region because the demographics were unsuitable. The wealthy population was composed of older, rather than very young, people interested in philanthropy.

Case Study 1: Success at Social Venture Partners Seattle

The David and Lucile Packard Foundation described the success of an SVP it funded in a report called *Transforming Philanthropic Transactions: An Evaluation of the First Five Years at Social Venture Partners Seattle*. The report indicated that over a five-year period, SVP Seattle worked with 35 nonprofits that focus on the fields of education, early childhood and the environment. In the course of a typical five-year relationship with an investee, the partnership invests approximately 200 to 300,000 dollars, provides ten to 20 strategic and hands-on volunteers, funds approximately 25,000 dollars worth of consultant support, and provides numerous connections to other information resources.[10]

The volunteer efforts of its partners are the backbone of SVP Seattle's capacity-building strategy. It has filled more than 350 volunteer assignments from its investees, over 200 of which also received strategic management assistance. The majority of the partners volunteered in technology and marketing, while some worked on financial management, strategic planning and other management functions.[11]

SVP Seattle's model for inspiring philanthropy is highly flexible. Partners make a 5,500 dollar annual commitment for two years and then choose from a range of activities. These might include attending partner education seminars, volunteering with investees, sitting on a grant committee, joining an internal working group, or simply receiving and reading the newsletter. None of these activities are required, although 75 percent of partners do more than write a check.[12]

Table 13.1
Social Venture Partners Seattle

Affilliate Stage	Partnerships	Investees	Investments (USD)	Investment Focus	Updated
Affilliate Stage					
SVP Arizona	126	19	$1,709,318	Children and Education	3.04
Austin SVP	30	20	$600,000	Children and Families in Austin	8.03
SVP Bay Area	28	9	$334,306	South of the Market Region, East Bay & the Peninsula	3.04
SVP Boston	25	7	$410,000	Economic Development	5.04
SVP Boulder Country	32	8	$375,000	Early Childhood & Youth Development	2.04
British Columbia Technology SVP	50	6	$170,000	Children, Women & East Downtown Vancouver	8.03
SVP Calgary	59	8	$457,060	Children and Education	3.04
Cleveland SVP	24	2	$120,000	Youth Development	3.04
Dallas SVP	50	9	$759,000	Children & Education	8.03
SVP Delaware	57	5	$467,000	Early Childhood Education	8.04
SVP Denver	47	5	$250,000	Elementary Education and Youth Development	8.03
SVP Minnesota	26	0		Children	8.03
Pittsburgh SVP	52	5	$300,000	At-Risk Children and Youth	3.04
SVP Portland	56	5	$260,000	Children & Education	8.03
San Diego SVP	52	6	$166,434	Improving the Quality of Life, Revolving Focus	8.03
SVP Seattle	270	38	$7,266,169	Education, Youth and Environment	3.04
St Louis SVP	37	3	$255,00	Youth and Children	1.04
Early Stage					
Baja SVP	8	0		TBD	12.03
SVP Chicago	10	0		Children and Education	8.03
Houston SVP	15	2	$100.00	Education & At-Risk Youth	8.03
Los Angeles SVP	15	0		TBD	7.04
SVP New Mexico	13	0		TBD	10.03
SVP Rhode Island	8	0		Social Enterprise Development	5.04
Totals	1097	157	$13,969,287		

The report also summarized the SVPs impact on its partners' philanthropy and volunteerism. Its findings include:

- Partners' interest in other types of philanthropic activities increased.
- Partners became more focused and strategic in their personal philanthropy.
- All partners increased their knowledge of community issues and nonprofit culture, which led many to become more willing to provide general operating support.
- Partners increased the quality and quantity of volunteering.
- Partners saw philanthropy and nonprofit work as a more significant part of their identity.
- Partners focused a greater portion of their philanthropic contributions on local organizations.
- An SVP association may counter people's inclination to reduce giving during economic downturns. (A number of SVP Seattle's most active partners said they actually increased their giving to local groups in the last year because they knew firsthand that it was needed more than ever.)[13]

Case Study 2: Success in Silicon Valley Social Venture Fund (SV2)

SV2 is a network of young professionals in the Silicon Valley region of California. The network promotes intelligent, active and effective giving to nonprofit organizations. The donation categories included:

- Founding Partner - $25,000 annually for two years
- Sustaining Partner - $12,500 annually for two years
- Partner - $5,000 annually for two years
- Initial Partner - $2,500 annually for two years[14]

The overall partner benefits are:

- The board matching program encourages SVP members to learn about the responsibilities of being nonprofit board members and helps them connect with nonprofits looking for leadership.
- Philanthropic Forum partners attend forums to learn about dynamic nonprofits and donor investment opportunities.

- The partnership provides an opportunity to invest intellectual and financial capital to increase the quality of services that nonprofits provide to the community.
- The partnership provides an opportunity to network and share one's charitable involvement with peers, friends and family, explaining which charities one supports and why.
- The partnership makes available educational seminars with peers, leading philanthropic speakers and professionals. These seminars offer opportunities to discuss different types of giving strategies, setting up funds, future trends in philanthropy and more.
- The partnership allows the donor to add his or her gift to a pooled fund with those of other partners so that the organization is able to give larger grants that provide more impact to the community.
- Partners can attend membership-building receptions throughout the year.
- The partnership offers opportunities to serve on SV2 committees: Grant Team, Impact Team, Technology Team, Inform and Educate Team.[15]

Starting an SVP

According to Social Venture Partners International (SVPI) in Seattle, an organization that helps new groups form SVPs, "Creating any new venture is an exciting, time consuming and complex process. Starting an SVP is no exception. Based on the experience of individuals and groups who have thought about or started an SVP, there are ten questions to ask during the 'idea stage.' The more 'yes' answers to these questions, the better.

1. Will an SVP fill a niche in my community?
2. Do I have connections to several existing SVP affiliates?
3. Do I have connections with a core group of business and/or philanthropy leaders in the community? (Founding boards need four to ten members. These people will play a leadership role in 'getting others into the game' as well.)
4. Do the members of the founding board have the time and patience for this? (At least two founding members will need to spend a minimum of ten hours

per week for six months or more.)

5. Do I have access to $50,000 to $100,000 in seed money and a plan for long-term sustainability beyond this initial funding? (To ensure durable growth and success, an SVP should aim for 25 partners in the first year.)

6. Do I fully understand the SVP model? (It is important to understand that the SVP involves a greater level of commitment than other 'giving circle' models.)

7. Can I make a one to three year commitment? Am I willing to use business and personal contacts to grow my SVP?

8. Do I want the SVP to be my primary community involvement? (Starting an SVP is like starting any other new business.)

9. Am I already involved in and familiar with the key issues in my community?

10. Has the funding board already agreed to approach the work in the community as a humble group of servant leaders who will learn from their partnerships with nonprofits? (One should think about the work as helping nonprofits strengthen themselves.)"[16]

SVPI of Seattle also notes that the Key Success Factors are
- Led by business, supported by community
- Sufficient seed capital
- Clear understanding of SVPs uniqueness
- Diverse representation
- Shared ownership of resources
- Access to SVPI resources/network
- Capture aspirations of partners.[17]

For those interested in starting a social venture partnership, SVPI will provide sample income and expense statements, and cash flow models for the first four years. They start with the assumption that 20 partners will give 5,000 dollars the first year, and the partnership will also receive a 100,000-dollar foundation grant and 80,000 dollars in angel or corporate support. Next, they can reasonably expect to hire an executive or program director at 63,000 dollars a year and an intern or graduate fellow at 2,000 dollars a year. These are all the customary expenses of a new charity or business–totaling 81,200 dollars. From this beginning, they can expect to give 26,667 dollars in grants the first year. By the second year, 50 partners could each give 5,000 dollars, with total donations amounting to 250,000 dollars. Foundation support would go down to 50,000 dollars and corporate sponsors down to 15,000 dollars. Expenses would then total 125,291 dollars. Grants would again total 26,667 dollars, plus another 65,557, dollars or a total of 93,333 dollars.[18]

In the third year, 75 partners could each give 5,000 dollars (300,000 dollars total). Grants would total 193,333 dollars. In the fourth year, 100 partners would each give 5,000 dollars (for a total of 500,000 dollars). The partnership is then able to issue 300,000 dollars in grants.[19]

A close look at the expenses of an SVP compared to a private foundation shows that the expenses are almost 40 percent of revenue received. In other words, by the fourth year, the expenses are 152,000 dollars a year and grants issued total 300,000 dollars. Now, there is always an operating fund for future promises, but this is a very expensive model to operate. It is important to note that this model is an educational program for future philanthropists. But, unless the demographics for the area include lots of wealthy young people, the model might not be workable. (For detailed advice on setting up an SVP, visit "Welcome to SVP-in-a-Box" online.)

To summarize, success in social venture partnership relationships is most likely to occur with the presence of:

- A committed source for the seed money to cover administrative costs for identifying needs and the constituency that is to contribute
- A large, local, young wealthy constituency who successfully created their own wealth
- A community foundation that has established a priority to help young, wealthy people develop skills in philanthropy
- A significant number of local charities that would welcome a relationship with a "managing partner," and would willingly accept changes in the way they operate along with the money investment.

14

ESTABLISHING A NON-CASH GIFT POLICY

Cash is king, and gifts of cash are easy to accept. But often a non-cash gift is commonly significantly beneficial to a charitable organization that has advisors who understand the true value of the gift. Conversely, some non-cash gifts become liabilities. So, it is essential for fund-raising leaders to understand the potential of the many types of non-cash gifts.

Real Estate

Real estate can be a wonderful gift, especially if it can be used for the purposes of the charity. However, a real estate gift can pose problems. For example, the property might be contaminated and the cost of bringing it up to environmental compliance could be higher than the property's worth. Liens against the property or impending lawsuits can also make real estate a liability. Appropriate financial research and a title search should make the status of the real estate clear.

> The manner of giving is worth more than the gift.
>
> Pierre Corneille

A partial or minority interest in the real estate is another problem. If there is positive cash flow, it could be all right, but no cash flow creates liability. An objective real estate advisor can lay out the issues.

Publicly Traded Stock

For a donor who is looking for a tax deduction, publicly traded stocks and bonds are as good as cash. They are valued on the effective date of the gift regardless of whether the charitable organization chooses to hold them or sell them. The donor may endorse the stock certificates to the organization and get a tax deduction for the market value of the tax without paying state and federal capital gains tax. If the stock has been held a long time and is highly appreciated, the tax savings can be significant. The good news for the organization is that the direct gift without tax payments results in a larger gift to the service agency. Of course, financial office personnel must ensure that the proper endorsements are made on the investment documents so ownership is properly transferred.

If, on the other hand, the publicly traded stock is lower in value than its original price, the owner is probably better off selling it herself, taking a tax loss and donating the proceeds to the agency. Competent tax counsel for the donor will advise which course of action is best.

Hopefully, the organization has a variety of estate planning attorneys and accountants who fully understand the ramifications of non-cash gifts for both the donor and charity. And, if the prospective donor does not have such counsel, it would be a great service to both sides to provide her with some references and/or introduce her to the appropriate professionals.

Privately Held Stock

A significant number of very wealthy people derive their wealth from a privately held company. While the stock can be very valuable, it often has restrictions on changing hands.

While a stockholder may donate some of her stock in a privately held company to a charity, as permitted by the stockholder's agreement, there can be no written agreement that the corporation or another stockholder will buy it back. This could lead to problems. For instance, the charity may find that it owns stock in a company but has no voice on the board or with management. In this case, the charity may offer to sell the stock to other shareholders and the company, only to find that no one chooses to buy it or they offer only pennies on the dollar. This can create a very delicate situation.

Many organizations will not accept stock in a privately held company, but each situation is different. The agency's professional advisors can help evaluate whether there is any merit in accepting such a gift.

Other Real Property

Occasionally, the human service agency needs some very specific items, and a corporation is in a position to give things such as computers, office equipment or their manufactured products. Agency personnel must be aware that there is a significant difference between the tax deduction an individual can take and the one to which a corporation is entitled. The individual can deduct market value for most donated items, but a corporation can only deduct its basis. In other words, if the corporation gives computers that have already been depreciated, it gets no tax deduction because the equipment was recorded in their books at zero or a minimal amount below market value. In situations where a corporation gets no economic benefit, it is extremely important to give significant recognition because the organization is giving out of a desire to provide community support.

Since individuals are entitled to the market value as a deduction, a used computer's market value would be the price at which the piece could be sold in the used office equipment market. There is, however, one sticky issue. If the organization chose to sell the piece of equipment for only ten dollars, while the donor claimed a 200-dollar deduction, the IRS would probably take the position that the donor was only entitled to a ten-dollar deduction. If, on the other hand, the organization used the equipment for its own operations, the donor could probably get the 200-dollar market value deduction. Actually, most charities will not assign a value to donated real property. They usually put the weight of that decision on the donor.

> Money is like manure; it's not worth a thing unless it's spread around encouraging young things to grow.
>
> Thornton Wilder

Property of significant value may require special attention. The donor or the organization may choose to have an appraiser determine its worth. But, the issue is complex. Traditionally, an appraisal sought by a seller comes in higher than one sought by a buyer. Some appraisals value items at their lowest, or liquidation, value (the amount it would be sold for in bankruptcy or other circumstances requiring a forced sale). Others value items at their highest, or replacement, value (also called market value, the amount a buyer is willing to pay the seller).

But, the IRS is very wary of inflated appraisals from individuals giving gifts of property to public charities. If the gift is immediately sold, there is no question that the market value is at least what the item was sold for. It is clearly deductible for the donor in that amount (minus the amount she would have paid for capital gains, if applicable). This is not true if the same gift is made to a private foundation. A gift to a foundation merits a deduction based only on what the donor paid for it (the donor's basis) or the amount she inherited it as (the beneficiary basis). This is one of the major benefits of being a public charitable organization that has 501(c)3 status. The organization often offers a potential donor the best opportunity for maximum chartitable deductions. But, it is also the reason the feederal government holds 501(c)3 organizations to very high standards.

If the gift is given to a public charity for its charitable purpose, such as a building that will be a group home for an organization that operates residential programs, then the donor will get the full market value as the deduction. (There is no reduction for capital gains.) But, if the donor gives an item to the agency that does not serve a programing purpose, her deduction could be one of two amounts. Depending on the circumstances, the deduction would be either the market value less the amount she paid for capital gains, or only her cost basis. For example, if the donor gives an art museum a piece of art that is worth 100,000 dollars, and the donor paid only 10,000 dollars for it, she gets a 100,000-dollar deduction. If she donated the same piece of art to a social service organization, she would get only a 10,000-dollar deduction, or the cost basis. An excellent book called *Tax Economics of Charitable Giving* is a great source for every conceivable example of charitable giving. It is clearly written and contains pertinent tables of treasury regulations and legal cases.

Since the laws and interpretations are constantly changing, issues that arise from non-cash gifts show how essential it is to have sophisticated tax counsel available for the charity. The same is true for a potential donor so she can avoid problems with the IRS.

15

PUTTING VOLUNTEERS TO WORK

In his book, ***Living, Leading and the American Dream***, John W. Gardner reflected on his fascination with proverbs and maxims as a means to communicate what is most important in life. Four-word proverbs such as "Easy come, easy go;" three-word proverbs like "Misery loves company," "Love is blind," and "Que sera, sera;" and two-word proverbs such as "Tempus fugits" and "Know thyself" led him to puzzle about what the one-word maxims for life would be. For years, he put this question to people: "Suppose you were allowed to communicate one word of advice to a young person living in the year 2500. What would it be? One word!" The first three words on the list below were almost universally nominated for top positions, and over time Gardner chose the following six as the top contenders.

Live	Be, experience, grow, sense, function as a healthy organism
Learn	At the heart of human behavior
Love	Fraternal, sexual, religious, humanistic
Think	Understand, know
Give	Help, serve, share, care
Laugh	Smile, play, enjoy
Aspire	Try for something better[1]

Learning to Believe

The first step in teaching anyone how to ask for contributions is to have the right frame of reference. What, exactly, is the agency asking him to do? Interestingly, Gardner's maxims create that frame of reference. The agency is offering the volunteer an opportunity to live, learn, love, think, give, laugh and aspire. The key is a development department that also firmly believes in the importance of the opportunity to give. Without that conviction, the staff cannot teach others.

Learning to Articulate

The second step in teaching people how to ask for contributions is to find out why they care about the cause. Asking a person directly actually helps him articulate why he believes in it and wants to help. This knowledge is also essential when making a request to a potential donor.

Learning to Contribute

The third step is to ask volunteers what they are able to contribute to the project they have been asked to work on. They should not ask others for a contribution until they have already given because they cannot effectively ask others to give until they have done so themselves. This very real practice helps them understand the feeling of satisfaction that comes from giving to a worthy cause, in addition to helping them persuade someone else.

Learning to Ask

The fourth step is teaching people how to ask others. Some people have done it with some success in the past; others have been very successful; and some are reluctant to ask. A volunteer's level of experience or success will determine how effective he will be as a fund-raiser.

To train inexperienced or reluctant volunteers, the development department should hold a meeting with all of the volunteers. The focus should be the current project, and the presentation should be enthusiastic so all of the volunteers can be infected with the same fervor. In addition, staff should plan role playing exercises in whcih volunteers practice asking each other for a donation. If possible, experienced volunteers should be paired with new or less experienced ones. The feedback of those who have been successful in fund raising is invaluable, and their enthusiasm is contagious.

Planning and practicing what needs to be said is an important part of the training. In conversations with donors who are already familiar with the organization, volunteers should open the conversation by reaffirming that they have a common interest. Various sample scripts can be written for the volunteer to have in mind when he is talking. Once the volunteer elicits agreement about how valuable the work of the organization is, he should raise the subject of the need for money for a specific reason. Next, the potential donor should be thanked for her past support (assuming the development staff has done its homework and provided the volunteer with information about the prospective donor's past level of giving). The fund-raiser should then follow up by asking gently if it might be possible to make the same size gift or perhaps a larger gift this time. If the potential donor is unable to make a gift, the volunteer can conclude by thanking her again for past support and asking only that she keep the organization in mind.

> Donors don't give
> to institutions.
> They invest in ideas
> and people in whom
> they believe.
>
> G. T. Smith

Some volunteers will be more aggressive than others, just as some salespeople are. Development department staff should learn what the strengths of each one are and match volunteers with potential donors who would respond most positively to their unique style.

Identifying Volunteer Interests

Another important consideration is discovering what volunteers are most keenly interested in. They do their best work on the projects and programs about which they are most enthusiastic. If that happens to be special events, the development staff should give them that assignment. If they would be more helpful in asking for major contributions, the staff should ask them to contact potential donors who can either underwrite specific portions of the special event, or give a large contribution for a project. For example, if the largest level of contribution for the event is currently 5,000 dollars, the development department can create one for 10,000, 25,000 or 50,000, name it the Golden Angel and let the volunteer make the necessary contacts. Or, if the volunteer's area of interest is furnishing group homes, the staff could supply her with a list of all agency furnishing needs. The volunteer could approach large retailers for carpeting, appliances, furniture, linens and other necessities.

One special difficulty human service agencies face is that certain expenses arise for very unglamorous things–items and services that are essential but cannot be funded by grants. It can be very difficult to match those needs with what donors want to accomplish through their gifts. Such problems can frequently be solved by asking for suggestions and help from volunteers.

> Complete possession
> is proved
> only by giving.
> All you are unable
> to give
> possesses you.
>
> Andre Gide

Matching Volunteers with Donors

Whether they are existing donors or prospective donors, one of the most sensitive areas in fund raising is who asks whom because raising money is all about relationships. Two elements to consider are who is most likely to be successful and who is willing.

People are more likely to give when asked by someone they know or trust and respect, or with whom they share a mutual interest. And, the greater the familiarity and respect, the greater the chances are that the gift will be generous. Again, that is why it is so helpful to have high profile, well-respected leadership in a campaign.

People also trust those who have had similar experiences. In one instance, a very shy lady had agreed to help in fund raising for the Boy Scouts. She was a den mother, and her son was an Eagle Scout. A very high-ranking executive in a major corporation, who lived in another city, had also been an Eagle Scout. It was decided that this den mother would be the one to approach him. She got an appointment with the help of the development staff and went to see the man, accompanied by the executive director. They talked about the efforts of the Boy Scouts in that city, and it was a very pleasant conversation. But the executive was not buying in too enthusiastically.

Finally, the shy little lady said in a relatively timid voice, "Do you think your Boy Scout experience contributed to your success in the corporate world?"

"Well, yes," he answered, and began to enumerate specific areas.

"Then perhaps," said the lady, "you would consider helping us help more boys to have some of the same opportunities." The result was that they got a major personal contribution from the executive and another from the corporation. Clearly, the power of the request came from one who was volunteering.

Developing New Prospects

If the development department has identified a prospective donor who is able to make larger gifts, it is essential to find someone who knows that individual, if at all possible. Sometimes, the person is willing to contact the prospective donor and present the agency needs. At other times, the volunteer is only willing to provide the advantaged introduction.

Often, this is a sensitive issue. It is frustrating when a board member or committee member knows a prospective donor very well but refuses to ask for a contribution. The reason may be that there is a quid pro quo involved between the two people about asking each other for large contributions. In addition, the fear that "If I ask him to give to this, then he will ask me to give a similar sum to his favorite cause" often prevents a person from asking.

To break that barrier, the board member or volunteer should call her friend and say something like, "I'm very involved in ABC organization and think they do fine work. They would like to come and talk to you, and I would really appreciate it if you would give them that opportunity." Agency development staff then choose the most appropriate volunteer to ask for the donor's gift and a staff person who can accompany her. The staff person's role is at the meeting to talk in depth about the project and answer any questions the prospective donor might have. If the meeting is about a major contribution, the staff person should be the executive director. In other cases, a program director or the development director could provide the knowledge and authority required for the occasion.

Commending Volunteer Successes

Some volunteers are wonderful about drawing other people into the agency cause, while others are great about working in the program. Still others are good at asking for contributions. Agency staff should always give positive feedback to volunteers who are responsible for new contacts and contributions. When a new volunteer signs up, staff should say "thank you" to the person who brought her into the organization. Any time a volunteer asks for a gift and the check arrives, the staff should make sure the volunteer is notified and thanked. Gestures like these are what turn a good volunteer into a great one and keep her devoted to the agency's work. It is one more step in allowing people to experience the joy of giving, a feeling that is closely linked to the joy of living.

16

VOLUNTEER AND DONOR RECOGNITION

Well-managed human service agencies understand the importance of providing incentives and recognition to their employees, but they sometimes do not give the same consideration to their volunteers. This often results in difficulty recruiting and keeping volunteers and/or expanding their fund-raising efforts. The truth is that the most critical element in keeping a 501(c)3 organization in touch with its community is its volunteer constituency. Other funding sources also recognize the importance of volunteer participation and measure how well the service agency is accepted in the community by the number of volunteers, the number of hours worked, the amount of dollars contributed, and the amount of in-kind gifts.

> Appreciation can make a day–even change a life.
> Your willingness to put it into words is all that is necessary.
>
> Margaret Cousins

The contribution volunteers make to a service agency cannot be underestimated. These are the people who help move the work of the organization forward despite scarce resources. They do clerical work, help with clients, prepare food, host events, lend their professional care and artistic talents, give money, raise funds, and attract other resources to the service agency.

One definition of work is "productive activity for which you are materially compensated." So when an employee works in a salaried position, he receives a paycheck. The boss' pat on the back and peer recognition are bonuses. However, most volunteers offer their services because they want to help, and material compensation is not a factor. In fact, it usually costs volunteers money to help a chosen cause. They may incur a variety of expenses such as transportation, child care, elder care, meals eaten away from home, or purchasing treats for other volunteers or the people served. In addition, volunteers who are still working give up part of their productive time and frequently experience a loss in compensation as a result of time spent on committees, boards or direct volunteer work. All of these factors underscore why it is essential to recognize their gifts of time and energy.

Hosting a Recognition Event

Regular thank you letters, and verbal encouragement and appreciation are essential ways of offering well-deserved recognition. But, formal recognition of outstanding volunteers during a special event provides extra synergy. Not only does this method allow for public acknowledgement of volunteer contributions, it also helps solidify the organization's constituency by providing additional motivation to other volunteers.

The focus of the event should be on community–getting together and sharing a time of fellowship and appreciation for volunteers. Some service agencies also recognize outstanding employee achievement during the event. It is definitely important to include employees who also volunteer, such as the physical therapist who helps on fund-raising activities during his time off, or the clerical worker who volunteers in the recreation program on weekends.

Invitations

Event coordinators can send special letters to ten volunteers who will be receiving awards. Invitations should also be sent to all volunteers at least one month in advance of the event. If the event is to be underwritten by a sponsor, coordinators ought to include a return postcard for their response, and the name of the sponsor should be incorporated in the invitation. Table 16.1 shows a sample invitation.

Table 16.1

The Board of Directors
of ABC Organization
invites you
to a celebration of volunteers

on (date) at (time)
at (place).

In honor of your contributions,
all costs are underwritten by
(name of sponsor).

Types of Events

There is no right or wrong way to honor volunteers. Whether the event is simple or elaborate, it reflects the organization's willingness to thank those who have supported its mission and programs. The message is, "We salute you!"

Ideally, a recognition event is a luncheon or dinner that is totally underwritten by a sponsor at no cost to the participants. In some cases, a moderate ticket price is charged. This can be avoided if the event is a simple buffet supper prepared by a combination of willing staff members and volunteers or a community-minded caterer.

Often, volunteers do not feel that the agency should spend money to acknowledge them; therefore, the event can be an excellent opportunity for corporate sponsorship. For its part, the sponsoring corporation or business receives the benefit of being regarded as community-minded. Another way to save money is to host the event in the agency headquarters or one of its program sites. Another advantage to using agency space is that it helps keep people focused on the location and the work that they support. Another alternative is a nearby facility that reminds everyone "where we are," in terms of both the agency's culture and the surrounding community. For example, staff might choose a restaurant that reflects the agency's warm and friendly culture, or an outdoor location where memorable agency events are held. (It is important to have a strategy for cover due to inclement weather if an outdoor event is planned.)

Forms of Recognition for Service

Service pins, award plaques, diplomas, charm bracelets, engraved crystal, and pen and pencil sets are all examples of tokens used to say thank you. Unique awards made by members, clients or alumni of the organization can be used as well.

Service pins for years of service are often a big hit. The pins can be given for five-year increments. It is amazing how many people sport them on their lapels because they are proud of their long-term commitment. Pins are particularly meaningful at the community level when they are spotted by another person at a time or place not connected to the agency.

The person who presents the award is also significant. Of course, the advantages of having a celebrity emcee or professional announcer are numerous. A celebrity draws more attention to the event, and a professional speaker can keep the pace of the program lively with a minimum of shuffling papers, searching for awards, and heartfelt but time-consuming side comments. If it is difficult to keep the three-hour Academy Awards program interesting, imagine how difficult it is to keep this type of program interesting even though it may last only an hour.

The invited celebrity can be anyone and the announcer's job is to give the verbal commendation. However, the person actually handing out the awards should be the executive director, president, board chair or program director. Also, each recipient should be photographed with that VIP as she receives the award. In some cases, photographs may be taken as a group. For example, everyone who has served 25 years can be photographed together, though each should receive her award individually as her name is announced. If the announcer is a celebrity, she should be photographed with the major award recipients. Eight by ten photographs should be sent to all of the recipients, and a five by seven photograph should be sent to the recipient's local newspaper. Newspaper coverage spreads the word about the organization's work, lets people in the community know who is involved, and gives the honorees a very public "thank you."

Advertising the Event

Communicating regularly through a newsletter is basic protocol for a human service agency. It is also a handy way to advertise a volunteer recognition event. Personal phone calls or email communication is another effective way to let people know. The traditional concept of a "phone tree" is also a great way to notify people. One person gets a list of people to call, and each person she calls is also given a list of names. This reduces the workload on any one person, and offers a greater sense of involvement for those who are invited. The most active volunteers are often the ones making the phone calls, but staff should be involved as well to the extent that their schedules allow. Volunteers and staff should work together to prioritize who will call what set of people. And, they should give careful attention to how the invitation is extended. The key is not just inviting the person or mentioning that she is receiving an award; it is one human being saying to another, "We really hope you will be able to attend our celebration of accomplishments."

> He who allows his day
> to pass by
> without practicing
> generosity . . .
> breathes
> but does not live.
>
> Sanskrit proverb

It is very important to understand the acceptance level for different forms of communication by different generational groups. For example, if the target group is in the Baby Boomer or Generation X age category, email may work well for a majority of them. However, if the target group are individuals from the World War II generation, a letter or phone call may be a much more effective form of communication since a large percentage of that population are not email oriented. Follow-up phone calls and personal visits may elicit an even better response from this group.

If a donor or legislator has been a truly outstanding supporter of the agency, the date of the event might be based on a time when that person is available. Organizations that plan recognition events around an outstanding supporter and then schedule it during a time when the person is very busy (or worse, unavailable) appear most concerned about their own needs, not the VIP's needs.

What Is a Community Foundation?

A community foundation is a nonprofit organization that exists to oversee funds set up by members of its community and to make charitable grants to local people and organizations. About 450 community foundations exist in the United States. Think of them as pools of funds invested for the future of their communities.

Calling them "community foundations" is far from accidental since they focus on benefiting the local communities they serve and are unique products of these communities.

Donors who set up funds may be famous or obscure. They can be individuals, families and corporations–even casual groups of friends with a common charitable vision. Community foundations respond quickly and specifically to needs that develop at the local level, and they endow community priorities for decades into the future.

While each community foundation has its own distinct personality and style, all share several attributes:

- Each exists so that individuals and corporate or nonprofit organizations can establish a charitable fund without having to cope with the complexities of setting up a special-purpose nonprofit corporation.
- Each community foundation functions, in effect, as a philanthropic and grant-making collective. A unique characteristic is that community foundations make it possible for whomever establishes a fund to make certain the money serves specific charitable purposes. At the same time, however, a community foundation

Reprinted by courtesy of Ron Gother, president of the Desert Community Foundation.

pools all of its funds for investment purposes–making it possible for individual, small funds to achieve economies of scale. For example, a community foundation might make a single grant for development of low-income housing that includes money from half a dozen different individual funds focused on the same field.

- Each community foundation is headquartered in and serves a specific community–some as confined as a small city, others as large as entire states or regions within states. Accordingly, a community foundation is a locally managed organization with a fund base that reflects the priorities and the imperatives of the community itself.
- Some community foundations, like ours, operate resource libraries, providing service to nonprofit staff, boards and others in the community.

While a community foundation is a single entity made up of many financial parts–some small, others large–it enjoys expertise in financial management found only in larger philanthropic organizations. Similarly, a community foundation possesses expertise in grant-making otherwise known to large charities, but available to benefit even the smallest funds.

Desert Community Foundation
42-600 Cook Street, Suite 201B
Palm Desert, CA 92911
Phone: (760) 674-9080
FAX: (760) 674-8121

NOTES

Chapter 1

1. *Encyclopedia Britannica*, 14th ed., 1937, s.v. "Charity."

2. Ibid.

3. Ibid.

4. "Doing Well and Doing Good," *The Economist* (July 31, 2004): 57-59.

5. *American Heritage Dictionary of the English Language*, 1995, s.v. "Charity."

6. *American Heritage Dictionary of the English Language*, 1995, s.v. "Philanthropy."

7. Gross, lecture, Planned Giving Institute, College of William and Mary, Williamsburg, VA, October 4, 1993.

8. Gary and Kohner. *Inspired Philanthropy*, 4.

Chapter 2

1. Broce, *Fund Raising: The Guide to Raising Money from Private Sources*, 207.

2. Gardner, *Building Community*, 21.

3. Ibid., 22.

4. Lenoir (homily at Sacred Heart Church, Palm Desert, CA, and personal conversation, 2003).

5. Broce, *Fund Raising: The Guide to Raising Money from Private Sources*, 208-209.

6. Dove, *Conducting a Successful Fundraising Program*, 57.

7. Ibid.

8. Drucker, *Managing in a Time of Great Change*, 276.

Chapter 3

1. Brunner, *Time: Almanac 2000,* 313.

2. "Charities Brace for Shakeout," *The Chronicle of Philanthropy* (June 26, 2003): 6, 8.

3. Brunner, *Time: Almanac 2000,* 314.

4. U.S. Census Bureau 2000/Bureau of Labor Statistics, http://www.census.gov/main/www/cen2000.html (accessed March 15, 2002).

5. "Charities Brace for Shakeout," *The Chronicle of Philanthropy* (June 26, 2003): 6, 8.

6. Boudreau, "Donations Nationwide 2002: Giving Increased Slightly in 2002, Human Services Declined," *San Jose Mercury News,* sec. 1, June 23, 2003.

Chapter 5

1. Greenfield, *Fund-Raising Fundamentals: A Guide to Annual Giving for Professionals and Volunteers (Nonprofit Law, Finance and Management)*, 82.

2. Ibid., 47.

Chapter 6

1. "Advertising supplement," *The Chronicle of Philanthropy* (March 20, 2003): F6-F7.

2. "Fact Sheet: President Bush Signs Anti-Spam Law," The White House, www.whitehouse.gov/news/releases/2003/12/20031216-4.html (accessed October 2004).

3. "CAN-SPAM Regulations Will Have Little Impact on Charities," U.S. Public Policy Issues, Association of Fundraising Professionals, http://www.afpnet.org/tier3_ed.cfm?folder_id=2465&content_item_id=17967 (accessed October 2004).

4. Ibid.

5. Roberts, "It's Official – CAN-SPAM Is Law," Email Universe, (December 16, 2003), http://EmailUniverse.com (accessed October 2004).

Chapter 8

1. Gaudiani, "The Greater Good: How Philanthropy Drives the American Economy and Can Save Capitalism," *The Chronicle of Philanthropy* (October 2, 2003): 48.

2. "Doing Well and Doing Good," *The Economist* (July 31, 2004): 59.

3. Ibid.

4. The Foundation Center, "FC-Stats: Grantmaker Information," (June 2, 2003), http://fdncenter.org/fc_stats/grantmakerinfo.html (accessed October 2004).

5. Schwinn and Tumgoren, "The Megagift Plunge," *The Chronicle of Philanthropy* (February 20, 2003): 8-9.

6. Lewis and Murray, "Top Donors of 2003," *The Chronicle of Philanthropy* (February 19, 2004): 6-7, 18.

7. Kroll and Goldman, eds. "Survival of the Richest," *Forbes Magazine* (March 17, 2003): 87-144.

8. "America's Biggest Donors List 2002," *The Chronicle of Philanthropy* (February 20, 2003): 9.

9. "How Americans Give," *The Chronicle of Philanthropy* (May 1, 2003): 8.

Chapter 9

1. Nelson-Walker, *Planned Giving for Social Service Agencies*, 65.

2. "Highlights of the Foundation Center's *Foundation Yearbook*," (Foundation Series Edition 2003), 3, http://fdncenter.org/media/stats.html (accessed October 2004).

3. "Top 100 U.S. Foundations by Asset Size," The Foundation Center, http://fdncenter.org/research/trends_analysis/top100assets.html (accessed October 2004).

4. Wolverton, "No More Wiggle Room," *The Chronicle of Philanthropy* (March 6, 2003), http://philanthropy.com/free/articles/v15/i10/10000701.htm (accessed October 2004).

5. Snyder, "The 2002 Slate 60: Top Donations," *Slate* (Feb. 17, 2003), http://slate.msn.com/id/2078474 (accessed October 2004).

6. Tice, "Large Donor List Includes Three State Residents," *Puget Sound Business Journal* (March 15, 2004): 1.

7. "Highlights of the Foundation Center's *Foundation Yearbook*," 3.

Chapter 10

1. Nelson, *Creating Community Acceptance for Handicapped People*, 187.

Chapter 11

1. Dove, *Conducting a Successful Capital Campaign*, 72.

2. Ibid., 69.

3. Ibid., 70.

4. Ibid.

Chapter 12

1. AAFRC Trust for Philanthropy, *Giving USA 2003* (Indianapolis: AAFRC, 2003), http://www.aafrc.org/press_releases/charityholds.html (accessed October 2004).

2. Havens and Schervish, "Millionaires and the Millennium: New Estimates of the Forthcoming Wealth Transfer and the Prospects for a Golden Age of Philanthropy," (Boston: Boston College, Social Welfare Research Institute), http://www.bc.edu/research/swri/publication/by-year/publications-1999 (accessed October 2004).

3. Havens and Schervish, "Why the $41 Trillion Wealth Transfer Estimate Is Still Valid: A Review of Challenges and Questions," *The Journal of Gift Planning*, 7, 1 (January 2003): 15.

4. Ibid.

5. Ibid.

6. Ibid.

Chapter 13

1. Letts, Ryan and Grossman, "Virtuous Capital: What Foundations Can Learn from Venture Capitalists," *Harvard Business Review* (March 1997): 43.

2. Ibid.

3. Ibid.

4. Gose, "A Revolution Was Ventured, But What Did It Gain?" *The Chronicle of Philanthropy* (August 21, 2003), http://philanthropy.com/free/articles/v15/i21/21000601.htm (accessed October 2004).

5. Ibid.

6. *Social Venture Partners International Affiliate Snapshot* (Seattle, WA: SVPI, 2004). A chart.

7. "About Us" (Washington DC: Venture Philanthropy Partners, 2004), http://www.venturephilanthropypartners.org/about/index.html (accessed November 2004).

8. Walker, "School Fund Charters 2M Gift," *The San Francisco Business Times* (July 4, 2003): 1, http://sanfrancisco.bizjournals.com/sanfrancisco/sto-ries/2003/07/07/story8.html (accessed November 2004).

9. Morales, *Venture Philanthropy History and Starting an SVP Affiliate* (brochure, conference sponsored by Social Venture Partners International, Seattle, WA, 2004).

10. Guthrie, Preston, and Bernholz, *Transforming Philanthropic Transactions: An Evaluation of the First Five Years at Social Venture Partners Seattle*, 3-5.

11. Ibid.

12. Ibid.

13. Ibid., 4.

14. "Silicon Valley Social Venture Fund (SV2): Become a Partner," Silicon Valley Social Venture Fund, http://www.cfsv.org/sv2.html (accessed November 2004).

15. Ibid.

16. Morales, *Venture Philanthropy History and Starting an SVP Affiliate* (brochure, conference sponsored by Social Venture Partners International, Seattle, WA, 2004).

17. Ibid.

18. Ibid.

19. Ibid.

Chapter 15

1. Gardner, *Living, Leading and the American Dream,* 57-60.

REFERENCES

AAFRC Trust for Philanthropy. 2003. Giving USA 2003. Indianapolis: AAFRC. http://www.aafrc.org/press_releases/charityholds.html (accessed October 2004).

"Advertising supplement." 2003. *The Chronicle of Philanthropy* (March 20): F6-F7.

American Heritage Dictionary of the English Language. 3rd ed. 1996. Boston: Houghton Mifflin.

"America's Biggest Donors List 2002." 2003. *The Chronicle of Philanthropy* (February 20): 8-9.

Avery Robert B. and Michael S. Rendall. 1993. "Estimating the Size and Distribution of Baby Boomers' Prospective Inheritances." American Statistical Association, Proceedings of the Social Statistics Section.

Boudreau, John. 2003. "Donations Nationwide 2002: Giving Increased Slightly in 2002, Human Services Declined," *San Jose Mercury News,* sec. 1, June 23.

Broce, Thomas E. 1986. *Fund Raising: The Guide to Raising Money from Private Sources.* 2nd ed. Norman: University of Oklahoma Press.

Brunner, Borgna, ed. 2000. *Time: Almanac 2000.* Needham, MA: Information Please.

"CAN-SPAM Regulations Will Have Little Impact on Charities." U.S. Public Policy Issues, Association of Fundraising Professionals. www.afpnet.org/tier3_ed.cfm?folder_id=2465&content_item_id=17967 (accessed October 2004).

"Charities Brace for Shakeout." 2003. *The Chronicle of Philanthropy* (June 26): 6, 8.

"Doing Well and Doing Good." 2004. *The Economist* (July 31): 57-59.

Dove, Kent E. 2001. *Conducting a Successful Fundraising Program.* San Francisco: Jossey-Bass.

Drucker, Peter F. 1995. *Managing in a Time of Great Change.* New York: Truman Talley Books.

Encyclopedia Britannica, 14th ed. 1937. Chicago: Encyclopedia Britannica.

"Fact Sheet: President Bush Signs Anti-Spam Law." The White House. www.whitehouse.gov/news/releases/2003/12/20031216-4.html (accessed October 2004).

"FC-Stats: Grantmaker Information." The Foundation Center. http://fdncenter.org/fc_stats/grantmakerinfo.html (accessed June 2, 2003).

Gardner, John W. 1990. *Building Community.* New York: Free Press.

———. 2003. *Living, Leading and the American Dream.* San Francisco: Jossey-Bass.

Gary, Tracy, and Melissa Kohner. 1999. *Inspired Philanthropy.* Oakland: Chardon Press.

Gaudiani, Claire. 2003. "The Greater Good: How Philanthropy Drives the American Economy and Can Save Capitalism." *The Chronicle of Philanthropy* (October 2): 48.

Gose, Ben. 2003. "A Revolution Was Ventured, But What Did It Gain?" *The Chronicle of Philanthropy* (August 21). http://philanthropy.com/free/articles/v15/821/21000601.htm (accessed October 2004).

Greenfield, James M. 1994. *Fund-raising Fundamentals: A Guide to Annual Giving for Professionals and Volunteers (Nonprofit Law, Finance and Management).* New York: John Wiley.

Gross, Robert. 1993. Lecture, Planned Giving Institute, College of William and Mary, Williamsburg, VA.

Guthrie, Kendall, Alan Preston, and Lucy Bernholz. 2002. *Transforming Philanthropic Transactions: An Evaluation of the First Five Years at Social Venture Partners Seattle.* San Francisco: Blueprint Research & Design.

Havens, John J., and Paul G. Schervish. 1999. *Millionaires and the Millennium: New Estimates of the Forthcoming Wealth Transfer and the Prospects for a Golden Age of Philanthropy.* Boston: Boston College, Social Welfare Research Institute. www.bc.edu/research/swri/publication/by-year/publications-1999 (accessed October 2004).

Havens, John J., and Paul G. Schervish. 2003. "Why the $41 Trillion Wealth Transfer Estimate Is Still Valid: A Review of Challenges and Questions." *The Journal of Gift Planning,* 7, 1 (January): 15.

"Highlights of the Foundation Center's *Foundation Yearbook.*" Foundation Series Edition 2003. http://fdncenter.org/media/stats.html (accessed October 2004).

"How Americans Give Chart." 2003. *The Chronicle of Philanthropy* (May 1): 7-8.

Kroll, Luisa, and Lea Goldman, eds. 2003. "Survival of the Richest." *Forbes Magazine* (March 17): 87-144.

Lenoir, John. 2003. Homily at Sacred Heart Church, Palm Desert, CA, and personal conversation.

Letts, Christine, William Ryan and Allen Grossman. 1997. "Virtuous Capital: What Foundations Can Learn from Venture Capitalists." *Harvard Business Review* (March): 36-44.

Lev. 19:10.

Lewis, Nicole, and Matt Murray. 2004. "Top Donors of 2003." *The Chronicle of Philanthropy* (February 19): 6-7, 18.

Morales, Tammy. 2004. *Venture Philanthropy History and Starting an SVP Affiliate.* Brochure, conference sponsored by Social Venture Partners International, Seattle, WA.

Nelson, Roberta. 1978. *Creating Community Acceptance for Handicapped People.* Springfield: Charles C. Thomas.

Nelson-Walker, Roberta. 2002. *Planned Giving for Social Service Agencies.* Homewood: High Tide Press.

Roberts, Janet. 2003. "It's Official – CAN-SPAM Is Law." Email Universe (December 16). http://EmailUniverse.com (accessed October 2004).

Schwinn, Elizabeth, and Ziya Serdar Tumgoren. 2003. "The Megagift Plunge." *The Chronicle of Philanthropy* (February 20): 6-9.

Snyder, Laurie. 2003. "The 2002 Slate 60: Top Donations." *Slate* (February 17). http://slate.msn.com/id/2078474 (accessed October 2004).

Social Venture Partners International Affiliate Snapshot. 2004. SVPI. A chart.

Tice, Carol. 2004. "Large Donor List Includes Three State Residents." *Puget Sound Business Journal* (March 15), 1-2.

Toce, Joseph P., Jr. et al. 2004. *Tax Economics of Charitable Giving*. Valhalla: Warren, Gorham & Lamont.

"Top 100 U.S. Foundations by Asset Size." The Foundation Center. http://fdncenter.org/research/trends_analysis/top100assets.html (accessed October 2004).

U.S. Census Bureau 2000/Bureau of Labor Statistics. http://www.census.gov/main/www/cen2000.html (accessed October 2004).

"Who We Are." 2004. Silicon Valley Social Venture Fund. http://www.sv2.org/whoweare/index.html (accessed October 2004).

Wolverton, Brad. 2003. "No More Wiggle Room." *The Chronicle of Philanthropy* (March 6). http://philanthropy.com/free/articles/v15/i10/10000701.htm (accessed October 2004).

ABOUT THE AUTHOR

Roberta Nelson-Walker has been involved in fund raising for nonprofit agencies for thirty years as a volunteer, director of development and executive director. She helped establish several public charities, public support foundations and private foundations. She also worked in the financial sector with Prudential Insurance as a professional helping individuals and family-held businesses achieve their personal and financial goals.

Ms. Nelson-Walker has a master's degree in management of rehabilitation agencies from DePaul University. This book, her fifth, combines her experience as a financial service professional, executive, fund-raiser, volunteer and board member. It is specifically directed to help social service agencies capture the opportunity to gain future economic security by establishing the necessary structure for effective fund raising.

Ms. Nelson-Walker grew up in New York. She currently lives in Rancho Mirage, CA, is married to Clayton J. Klein, and has three married children and eight grandchildren. Her extended family includes Clay's two daughters, their husbands and nine grandchildren.